CIM REVISION CARDS
Marketing Research and Information

John Williams of Marketing Knowledge

ELSEVIER

AMSTERDAM • BOSTON • HEIDELBERG • LONDON • NEW YORK • OX
PARIS • SAN DIEGO • SAN FRANCISCO • SINGAPORE • SYDNEY • TO

Butterworth-Heinemann is an imprint of Elsevier
Linacre House, Jordan Hill, Oxford OX2 8DP
30 Corporate Drive, Suite 400, Burlington, MA 01803

First published 2006

British Library Cataloguing in Publication Data
A catalogue record for this book is available from the British Library

ISBN-13: 978 0 7506 8294 7
ISBN-10: 0 7506 8294 9

For information on all Elsevier Butterworth-Heinemann publications visit our website at http://books.elsevier.com

Printed and bound in Great Britain

06 07 08 09 10   10 9 8 7 6 5 4 3 2 1

TABLE OF CONTENTS

Preface..iv
1. Marketing research and information 1
2. Information in the knowledge economy 11
3. The marketing database 33
4. The marketing research process.. 61
5. Using secondary research.. 83
6. Observation research... 91
7. Qualitative research... 103
8. Quantitative data... 117
9. Questionnaire design... 131
10. Sampling 145
11. Quantitative data analysis.. 156
12. Presenting marketing research.. 172

PREFACE

Welcome to the CIM Revision Cards from Elsevier/Butterworth-Heinemann. We hope you will find these useful to revise for your CIM exam. The cards are designed to be used in conjunction with the CIM Coursebooks from Elsevier/Butterworth-Heinemann, and have been written specifically with revision in mind. They also serve as invaluable reviews of the complete modules, perfect for those studying via the assignment route.

■ Learning outcomes at the start of each chapter identify the main points

■ Key topics are summarized, helping you commit the information to memory quickly and easily

■ Examination and revision tips are provided to give extra guidance when preparing for the exam

■ Key diagrams are featured to aid the learning process

■ The compact size ensures the cards are easily transportable, so you can revise any time, anywhere

To get the most of your revision cards, try to look over them as frequently as you can when taking your CIM course. When read alongside the Coursebook they serve as the ideal companion to the main text. Good luck – we wish you every success with your CIM qualification!

MARKETING RESEARCH AND INFORMATION

INTRODUCTION

The Marketing Research and Information module has five major components:

- Information and research for decision-making
- Customer databases
- Marketing research in context
- Research methodologies
- Presenting and evaluating information to develop business advantage

Syllabus Reference: 1.1–1.4

INFORMATION AND RESEARCH FOR DECISION-MAKING

These elements of the syllabus relate to the role of information in the decision-making process within organizations and the management of marketing. Traditionally, marketers have used the marketing information system (MkIS) and its components to inform the decision-making process. Central to the process was the use of marketing research.

INFORMATION AND RESEARCH FOR DECISION-MAKING

The syllabus explores the background to and the development of information management and the growth of the 'information-based' economy. It links this to the way in which organizations should determine their marketing information requirements and how information users should specify their needs within the organization in order to drive profitable lasting relationships with customers. It covers the nature of the technical systems that are available to marketers to manage information and support decision-making.

Customer Databases

Syllabus Reference: 2.1–2.5

These elements of the syllabus cover the role of marketing databases in the management of Customer Relationship Management (CRM) systems. They look at the process of developing, maintaining and enhancing the customer database. It explores the role of customer and prospect profiling. It covers the vital role of data warehousing, data marts and data mining.

Example

TGI customer database

TGI is a research service run by BMRB. In this example it is run against an internal database and common characteristics identified.

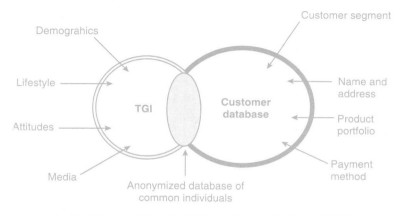

Demograhics

Lifestyle

Attitudes

Media

TGI

Customer database

Customer segment

Name and address

Product portfolio

Payment method

Anonymized database of common individuals

The First T Process TGI and the Database. Source: Clive Humby BMRB

Marketing Research in Context

Syllabus Reference: 3.1–3.6

The nature, size and scope of the market research industry, including the suppliers of research services and providers of database and other information services. The stages of a research programme and the procedures and briefing of external agencies.

The ability to get the best from suppliers is a key part of the manager's job and is also true for market research. Communicating a research problem and inspiring an agency to produce a thoughtful, well-structured research plan, is crucial to the process of decision-making.

The ethical and social responsibilities of the researcher, as laid down within the codes of conduct and legislation considerations.

Research Methodologies

These elements of the syllabus deal with the marketing research task and the methods that support the research process. They cover the range of methods and techniques that underpin good research design. Key capabilities include asking the right questions and using data to inform decision-making to reduce the risk to the business. Current techniques draw heavily on the internet, but there is a need to distinguish good from poor data.

The syllabus distinguishes between qualitative and quantitative research and the range of techniques that are used to gather this information; for example, questionnaires and topics guide design and delivery to support research design and analysis.

Presenting and Evaluating Information to Develop Business Advantage

Syllabus Reference: 5.1–5.3

This part of the syllabus looks at the evaluation and presentation of research data and its conclusions. It covers the techniques that are used in the analysis of quantitative and qualitative data and the production of written research reports and oral presentations of the results. The key aim of the module is to 'provide the knowledge and skills to manage marketing information, and the more specialist knowledge and skills required to plan, undertake and present results from market research' (CIM, 2003).

Related statements of marketing practice

These statements link the syllabus to the tasks of the marketing professional. The ones that apply to this module are:

- The evaluation of information requirements, the management of research projects and the marketing information system
- The evaluation and presentation of information for business advantage
- The ability to contribute information and ideas to the strategy process

➡ If you understand the learning outcomes of the module then you have a clear idea of what the examiners will be looking for in your assessment.

Learning Outcomes and Knowledge and Skills Requirements

Learning outcomes	Knowledge and skill requirements
Identify appropriate marketing information and market research requirements for business decision-making	1.1 Demonstrate a broad appreciation of the need for information in marketing and its role in the overall marketing process
	1.2 Explain the concept of knowledge management and its importance in the knowledge-based economy
	1.3 Explain how organizations determine their marketing information requirements and the key elements of user specifications for information
	1.4 Demonstrate an understanding of marketing management support systems and their different formats and components
Plan for and manage the acquisition, storage, retrieval and reporting of information on the organization's markets and customers	2.1 Demonstrate an understanding of the application, the role in CRM and the benefits of customer databases
	2.2 Describe the process for setting up a marketing database

Contd.

Learning outcomes	Knowledge and skill requirements
	2.3 Explain how organizations profile customs and prospects
	2.4 Explain the principles of data warehouses, data marts and data mining
	2.5 Explain the relationship between database marketing and marketing research
Explain the process involved in purchasing market research and the development of effective client supplier relationships	3.1 Describe the nature and structure of the market research industry
	3.2 Explain the stages of the market research process
	3.3 Describe the procedures for selecting a market research supplier
	3.4 Explain the ethical and social responsibilities inherent in the market research task
Write a research brief to meet the requirements of an organization to support a specific plan or business decision	3.5 Identify information requirements to support a specific business decision in an organization and develop a research brief to meet the requirements
Develop a research proposal to fulfil a given research brief	3.6 Develop a research proposal to fulfill a given research brief

Contd.

Learning outcomes	Knowledge and skill requirements
Evaluate the appropriateness of different qualitative and quantitative research methodologies to meet different research situations	4.1 Explain the uses, benefits and limitations of secondary data
	4.2 Recognize the key sources of primary and secondary data
	4.3 Describe and compare the various procedures for observing behaviour
Design and plan a research programme	4.4 Describe and compare the various methods for collecting qualitative and quantitative data
Design a questionnaire and topic Guide	4.5 Explain the theory and processes involved In sampling
	4.6 Design a questionnaire and discussion guide to meet a project's research objectives
Interpret quantitative and qualitative data, and present coherent and appropriate recommendations that lead to effective marketing and business decisions	5.1 Demonstrate an ability to use techniques for analyzing qualititative and quantitative data
	5.2 Write a research report aimed at supporting marketing decisions
Critically evaluate the outcomes and quality of a research project	5.3 Plan and design an oral presentation of market research reports

Source: CIM module two syllabus

Hints and Tips

- ■ Show the examiner that you understand the basis of the question, by answering precisely the question asked and not including just about everything you can remember about the subject area

- ■ Read their needs – How many points is the question asking you to address?

- ■ Respond to the question appropriately. Is the question asking you to take on a role? If so, take on the role and answer the question with respect of the role

- ■ Ensure the examiner has something to mark: give them substance, relevance, definitions, illustrations and demonstration of your knowledge and understanding of the subject area

- ■ Provide a strong sense of enthusiasm and professionalism in your answers; support it with relevant up-to-date examples and apply them wherever appropriate

- ■ Collect examples of the application of models, techniques, concepts, etc.

- ■ Make sure that you are able to apply your learning to actual marketing situations and issues

Go to www.cimvirtualinstitute.com and www.marketingonline.co.uk for additional support and guidance

INFORMATION IN THE KNOWLEDGE ECONOMY

- At the heart of successful enterprises is the effective management of information
- Integrated information is critical to effective decision-making. Advantage in the market place does not come just from carrying out research, it is about identifying, collating, understanding, analyzing and acting upon the many diverse sources of knowledge and information within an organization
- Many organizations are not organized to manage this process effectively

- The problem is not accessing information but analyzing it to produce intelligence upon which we can act
- To manage information effectively, many organizations need to undergo a significant cultural change. In particular, there is a need for cooperative and collaborative attitudes towards sharing it.
- However, many find this change difficult to manage. Information may exist in silos that are not connected, leading to critical gaps in understanding

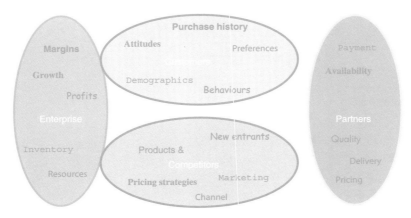

Figure 2.1 Multiple sources of data
Source: Teradata

A single view of the truth provides greater knowledge and insight (Figure 2.2).

Figure 2.2 The aim of knowledge management
Source: Teradata

Marketing Research (Dibb, Simkin, Pride and Ferrell, 2000)

Collection of marketing information

Answers the questions – What, where and when are customers buying?

- How do we compare with our competitors? etc.
- Why do customers respond to this form of sales promotion? etc.
- What would happen if the government introduced new legislation in this area, etc.

Typical data: market analysis

- Market profitability
- Market growth trends
- Main products in the market
- Customer attitudes and buying behaviours
- Major competitors and market shares
- Distribution patterns
- Marketing strategies used in the market

Typical data: product research

- New products
- Gap between current products and perception
- Consumer research
- Research from international markets
- Competitor research
- Long-range economic studies
- Satisfaction levels and trends with current products

Typical data requirements: pricing decisions

- Competitor product prices
- Consumer attitudes to price
- What would they expect to pay?
- What would they be prepared to pay?
- Cost price volume – what quantities are likely to sell at different price levels?

Typical data requirements: advertising and promotion

- Size of potential market
- Demographic characteristics of users
- Demographic profiles of segments
- Behaviours and attitudes of different segments
- Language used by customers in talking about product
- Share of mind compared with competitors

Typical data requirements: sales decisions

- Sales territories
- Sales personnel efficiency
- Sales statistics
- Sales forecasts
- Sales incentives

The knowledge age

- Huge volumes of information now available
- Managers need to be selective and systematic
- As data is drawn from multiple sources, it needs to be combined and analyzed for it to be of value

Knowledge management

- ■ The aim is to integrate systems and individuals to enable and encourage knowledge transfer between employees and other stakeholders
- ■ Knowledge involves organizing, interpreting and analyzing information to produce intelligence
- ■ Knowledge within organizations can take many forms:
    - ◆ Individual knowledge: resides in the mind of an individual
    - ◆ Organizational knowledge: interactions between technologies, techniques and people
    - ◆ Explicit knowledge: documented and shared through IT, externalized and conscious. Marketing research data is a good example of this type of knowledge
    - ◆ Tacit knowledge: hard to codify and document because individuals often take for granted what they know and how they do things. It can be difficult to communicate what they know in a form that others can use effectively

The Structure of an Information System

Technology infrastructure

Hardware

Systems software

Applications

Software

Communications

Personnel

Technology developers

Systems operators

Systems maintainers

Users

User support

Data infrastructure

Databases

Database management

Archiving communication

Marketing management support systems – The marketing information system (MkIS)

This is a system in an organization that supplies information, communication services and resources to meet organizational needs. The MkIS is the system used to put information at the heart of the decision-making process. A typical MkIS consists of four elements:

- The marketing research system is the backbone of the marketing information system
- The marketing intelligence system—published data existing in the market place
- The decision support system—contains the tools needed to make sense of data
- Internal records—includes e.g. sales and accounts records, details on past communications and the results of previous marketing research

The Marketing Information System (MkIS)

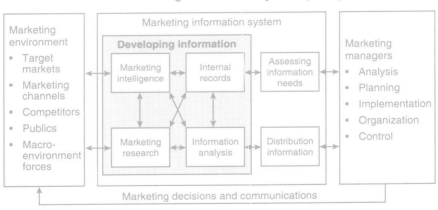

What is Marketing Research?

The Market Research Society (MRS) defines it as 'the collection and analysis of data from a sample of individuals or organizations relating to their characteristics, behaviour, attitudes, opinions or possessions. It includes all forms of marketing and social research, such as consumer and industrial surveys, psychological investigations, observational and panel studies' (MRS, 1999).

Marketing research is the function that links the consumer, customer and public to the marketer through information... it specifies the information required to address these issues, designs the method for collecting information, manages and implements the data collection process, analyzes the results, and communicates the findings and their implications (American Marketing Association, 2003).

Market research is a subset of marketing research. Market research refers to research on markets, whereas marketing research covers the broad scope of marketing activity.

Databases

A database does not have to be computer-based but access to database technology is easy and cheap. A database will collect data about past, potential and current customers. A database differs from an accounting system in that the data must be relevant to marketing decision-making. It is important that data fed into the marketing database is relevant to marketing decisions, now and in the future.

Wilson (2003) suggests that marketers develop customer databases for four reasons:

1. To personalize marketing communications
2. To improve customer service
3. To understand customer behaviour
4. To assess the effectiveness of the organization's marketing and service activities

Table 2.1 World Market Research Turnover and Growth Rates by Region 2004

Region	Turnover in million US$	Turnover in million US$	Turnover in million US$	Growth rate % (unadj. for inflation)**	Real growth rate % (adj. for inflation)**
	2002	2003	2004	2003/04	2003/04
EU15	6327	7590	8827	5.2	3.0
New member states	191	249	299	10.5	6.0
Other Europe	368	454	534	10.7	6.1
Total Europe	6885	8293	9660	5.6	3.2
North America	6707	7137	7853	9.5	6.7
Central and South America	632	720	830	14.8	8.2
Asia Pacific	239	2526	2863	6.5	5.2
Middle East & Africa	205	251	294	8.6	6.3
Total World	16 668	18 928	21501	7.5	5.0

* Some 2003 figures revised since 2003 industry Report published last year
** Growth rates are based on turnover in local currencies for 2003 and 2004 converted into dollars using 2004 exchange rate; real growth adjusted using the local inflation rate for 2004 (*Source:* IMF)
Source: ESOMAR Market Research Industry Survey 2004

Who Carries out Research?

Alan Wilson (2003) identifies the following:

- **List brokers** – Suppliers of lists of contacts for marketing purposes. They may include names and addresses, telephone numbers and e-mail addresses
- **Full service agencies** – Agencies that provide a full range of research services, e.g. TN Sofres
- **Specialist service agencies** – Specialize in certain types of research, e.g. international research or online research
- **Field agencies** – Specialize in the delivery of fieldwork and administration of questionnaires
- **Data analysis companies** – Specialize in the analysis of data
- **Consultants** – Independent consultants who may offer a range of services
- **Other suppliers** to the industry include database bureaus who may host an external database

Who Carries out Research?

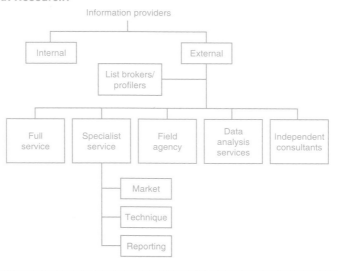

Leading global research companies carry out research using a variety of research techniques. The table shows the split between techniques.

Type of research	%
Face-to face interviews	32.9
Telephone interviews	19.5
Discussion groups	8.8
Consumer panels	8.3
Postal/self-completion	8.0
Hall/central location test	7.7
Retail audits	4.5
In-depth interviews	3.6
Street interviews	2.0
Observation	0.3
Web/Internet interview	0.2

Percent Research Turnover by Method 2002. *Source*: BMRA (2002)

Internal secondary research: sources

- Sales figures
- Operational data – stock levels, etc.
- Customer satisfaction results
- Advertising spend
- Customer complaints records
- Effectiveness data from promotional campaigns
- Marketing research reports from past studies

External secondary research: sources

- Internet – single search engines and multiple search engines
- Directories
- Country information
- Published marketing research reports
- News sources and discussion lists

Ethics, regulation and codes of practice in market research

The 'data' industry has grown rapidly as the technology that is available to capture, store analyze and exchange data has improved. The amount of data held on individuals is vast and increasing. This raises many issues

Data protection

The UK Data Protection Act regulates 'processing' of data; this covers data on any living person and there are separate rules for sensitive data. The guiding principles in the Act are transparency and consent. Individuals must have a clear understanding of why their data is being captured and what it will be used for, and they must consent to its use and be given the opportunity to opt out of any later use of this data

Codes of practice

Not legally binding but do represent good practice, and members of the professional bodies must comply with the code of conduct. The MRS code of conduct is available at www.mrs.org.uk. You should download this and add it to your study materials

UK Data Protection Act

8 Key Principles:

1. Data processing must be done fairly and lawfully. Information about the organization gathering information must be given and consent from data subjects must be obtained

2. Data must be obtained only for specific and lawful purposes, and shall not be further processed in a manner incompatible with that purpose

3. Personal data must be adequate, relevant and not excessive in relation to the purposes for which it is processed

4. Personal data must be accurate and where necessary up to date, with every reasonable step taken to ensure this

5. Personal data should not be kept for longer than is necessary

6. Personal data shall be processed in accordance with the data subjects' rights

7. The data must be kept secure against accidental loss, destruction or damage. The collector of the data must have a written contract with the data processor who may process data on behalf of the controller guaranteeing security

8. Overseas transfer of data, should not be outside the European Economic Area (EEA), EU plus Norway, Iceland and Liechtenstein, unless consent is given. If data is exported, it must be to countries approved by the information commissioner. Hungary, Switzerland, New Zealand and Canada are the only ones that qualify at present

Summary

- Marketing is the management process responsible for identifying, anticipating and satisfying customer needs profitably means that timely, accurate and pertinent information underpins marketing orientation

- The MkIS is the mechanism for delivering this information, and Marketing Research and the Database are the key components of this system

- Marketing research is the collection and analysis of data from a sample of individuals or organizations relating to their characteristics, behaviour, attitudes, opinions or possessions. It includes all forms of marketing and social research such as consumer and industrial surveys, psychological investigations, observational and panel studies

- The database is 'a manual or computerized source of data relevant to marketing decision making about an organization's customers' (Wilson, 2003). It can be enhanced by other data, including geo-demographic and lifestyle data

- The industry works within a legislative and self-regulatory environment which includes the Data Protection Act, the Freedom of Information Act and the MRS and ICC/ESOMAR codes of practice

Hints and Tips

- ■ The marketing information system provides a useful way of storing information and making sense of it
- ■ Information is available in vast quantities and managers need to be able to select what is and is not useful. The problem is not so much accessing information, but analyzing it effectively and efficiently to produce actionable intelligence
- ■ Database systems are not just useful in storing and analyzing customer information, but can play a part in helping to organize marketing information needs
- ■ Competitive intelligence is a specific form of Market Intelligence. This is often undertaken on an on-going basis and involves the collection of news, materials and other information about competitors from a wide variety of sources. Competitive intelligence is more about putting structures in place than specifically finding one-off pieces of data
- ■ Don't overlook knowledge about customers, markets and competitors that comes from staff. Often this is a poorly tapped source of information. Collecting and disseminating such information falls into the realms of customer knowledge management and making better use of customer knowledge can help businesses focus on what the customer wants and says

Go to www.cimvirtualinstitute.com and www.marketingonline.co.uk for additional support and guidance

THE MARKETING DATABASE

Syllabus Reference: 2.1–2.5

After completing this unit you will:

- Be able to define the marketing database and its role within Customer Relationship Management systems
- Understand the marketing applications supported by the marketing database
- Understand the management process involved in building, maintaining and enhancing the database
- Understand and define the concepts of data warehouses and data mining

Key definitions

Attributed data	Data that is extrapolated from the results of market research
Behavioural data	Data that is derived directly from the behaviour of the customer
Data capture	Information taken on to a computer system
De-duplication	System of removing names and addresses which appear in a list more than once
Geo-demographics	Companies supply a system of categorizing the country into a number of different demographic types. Each postcode in the country is assigned one of these types. This means that each customer on a database can be matched to a demographic type. When this is done across customer records, a demographic profile emerges
Golden fields	The key information elements of the database that must be completed and maintained for good database marketing
Lifestyle data	Lifestyle companies collect information on customers' lifestyles. The data is assembled from various sources; guarantee cards filled in, in return for an extended warranty
OLAP	On Line Analytical Processing
Profile data	Data that is obtained by linking the database with other sources of information
Volunteered data	Data that is given up by the customer through, e.g. registering on a website

Customer relationship management

CRM is an integrated approach to identifying, acquiring, and retaining customers. It enables organizations to manage and coordinate customer interactions across multiple channels, departments, lines of business, and geographically.

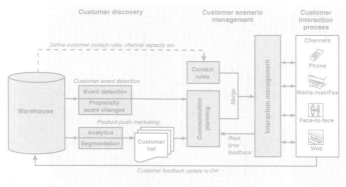

CRM and Data Warehousing. Source: Teradata

Geo-Demographic and Lifestyle Profiling.

Data can be enhanced through overlaying bought-in data. Data can be bought from, e.g. Experian, who runs the Mosaic system, CACI, who runs ACORN and Claritas, who runs a number of lifestyle overlays.

Visit the following websites:

www.experian.com

www.claritas.co.uk

www.caci.co.uk

- Lifestyle classification works normally on researched lists. Acxiom, for example, collects data from the warranty registration cards for domestic appliances filled in by new customers
- Geodemographics works on the idea that 'birds of a feather flock together' and that customers who share postcodes will share behavioural characteristics
- Mosaic divides households in the country into 11 groups and 61 types. The Mosaic classification is based in large part on census data but also includes other data sources. According to MOSAIC 54 percent of the data used to build Mosaic is sourced from the 2001 Census. The remaining 46 percent is derived from their Consumer Segmentation Database, which provides coverage of all of the UK's 46 million adult residents and 23 million households

It includes:

- The edited Electoral Roll
- Experian Lifestyle Survey information, and Consumer Credit Activity
- The Post Office Address File
- Shareholders Register
- House Price and Council Tax information
- ONS local area statistics

Source: www.business-strategies.co.uk/

The Mosaic system's 11 groups are as follows:

- Symbols of Success
- Happy Families
- Suburban Comfort
- Ties of Community
- Urban Intelligence
- Welfare Borderline
- Municipal Dependency
- Blue Collar Enterprise
- Twilight Subsistence
- Grey Perspectives
- Rural Isolation

Other geo-demographic systems work in a similar way. For example, ACORN

THE ACORN CONSUMER CLASSIFICATION

CATEGORY		% UK POP	GROUP		% UK POP
1	WEALTHLY ACHIEVERS	25.1	A	WEALTHLY EXECUTIVES	8.6
			B	AFFLUENT GREYS	7.7
			C	FLOURISHING FAMILIES	8.8
2	URBAN PROSPERITY	10.7	D	PROSPEROUS PROFESSIONALS	2.2
			E	EDUCATED URBANITES	4.6
			F	ASPIRING SINGLES	3.9
3	COMFORTABLY OFF	26.6	G	STARTING OUT	2.5
			H	SECURE FAMILIES	15.5
			I	SETTLED SUBURBIA	6
			J	PRUDENT PENSIONERS	2.6

Figure 3.1. The Acorn consumer classification

Contd.

4	MODERATE MEANS	14.5	K	ASIAN COMMUNITIES	2.5	
			L	POST-INDUSTRIAL FAMILIES	15.5	
			M	BLUE-COLLAR ROOTS	6	
5	HARD-PRESSED	22.4	N	STRUGGLING FAMILIES	14.1	
			O	BURDENED SINGLES	4.5	
			P	HIGH-RISE HARDSHIP	1.6	
			Q	INNER CITY ADVERSITY	2.1	
			U	UNCLASSIFIED	0.3	

Contd.

GROUP	TYPE		% UK POP
A	1	Wealthy mature professionals, large houses	1.7
	2	Wealthy working families with mortages	1.5
	3	Villages with wealthy commuters	2.7
	4	Well-off managers, larger houses	2.6
B	5	Older affluent professional	1.8
	6	Farming communities	2.0
	7	Old people, detached homes	1.9
	8	Mature couples, smaller detached homes	2.0
C	9	Older families, prosperous suburbs	2.1
	10	Well-off working families with mortages	2.3
	11	Well-off managers, detached homes	3.7
	12	Large families and houses in rural areas	0.6
D	13	Well-off professionals, large houses and converted flats	0.9
	14	Older professionals in suburban houses and apartments	1.4
E	15	Affluent urban professionals, flats	1.1
	16	Prosperous young professionals, flats	0.9
	17	Young educated workers, flats	0.6
	18	Multi-ethnic young converted flats	1.1
	19	Suburban privately renting professionals	0.9
F	20	Students flats and cosmpoliton shares	0.6
	21	Single and shares, multi-ethnic areas	1.6
	22	Low income singles, small rented flats	1.2
	23	Student terraces	0.4
G	24	Young couples, flats and terraces	1.0
	25	White-collar singles/shares, terraces	1.4
H	26	Young white-collar couples with mortages	1.9
	27	Middle income, home owning areas	2.9
	28	Working families with mortages	2.6
	29	Mature families in suburban semis	3.3
	30	Established home owning workers	3.6
	31	Home owning Asian family areas	1.1

Contd.

I	32	Retired home owners	0.9
	33	Middle income, older couples	3.0
	34	Lower incomes, older people, semis	2.1
J	35	Elderly singles, purposes built flats	0.7
	36	Older people, flats	1.9
K	37	Crowded Asian terraces	0.5
	38	Low income Asian families	1.1
L	39	Skilled Older families, terraces	2.8
	40	Young working families	2.1
M	41	Skilled workers, semis and terraces	3.3
	42	Home owning families, and terraces	2.8
	43	Older people, rented terraces	1.8
N	44	Low income larger families, semis	3.3
	45	Low income, older people, smaller semis	3.0
	46	Low income, routine jobs, terraces and flats	1.4
	47	Low income families, terraced estates	2.6
	48	Families and single parents, semis and terraces	2.1
	49	Larger families and single parents, many children	1.7
O	50	Single elderly people, council flats	1.8
	51	Single parents and pensioners, council terraces	1.9
	52	Families and single parents, council flats	0.8
P	53	Old people, many high-rise flats	0.8
	54	Singles and single parents, high-rise estates	0.9
Q	55	Multi-ethnic purpose built estates	1.1
	56	Multi-ethnic, crowded flats	1.1
U	57	Mainly communal population	0.3

The Process of Setting Up a Marketing Database

The process of setting up a database is complex and demanding.

Stages

- Business review
- Data audit
- Data strategy, specification and verification
- Data verification
- Hardware/software
- Data capture, maintenance and enhancement
- Management issues – should the database be run in-house/out-house
- Applications
- Review

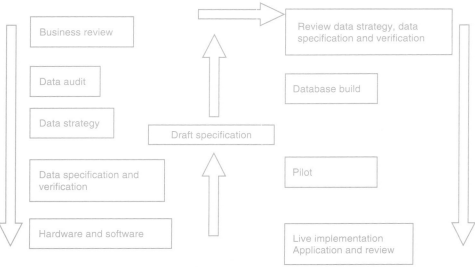

Figure 3.2 The database development process

Business Review

All business decisions should begin with an understanding of the strategic direction of the business. The following questions need to be asked:

- How will data help the business achieve its business and marketing objectives?
- Where will the business be in 10 years' time?
- What media, information and technology changes will need to be built into the system?
- What business processes will the database support?
- How will the database be accessed?

The Data Audit

The following needs to be established:

- What information requirements does the organization have now and in the future?
- Where is this information held currently?
- How is this information currently used?
- How will it be used in future?
- Which departments and individuals need access to this information?
- If information is not available, where does it come from?
- Who will enter the data and ensure that it is accurate and complete?
- What applications will this information support?
- How does the proposed system integrate with existing information management systems?

Review of Strategy and Data Audit

The review of strategy and the data audit should result in a long-term strategy for data within the organization. This should be capable of evolution and development over time as the markets served by the organization, and the organization itself, changes. The strategy should specify the information that is required by the organization, outlining where the information is available and what additional data is to be acquired and managed.

It should determine the following:

- Who and what departments are able to use and update data held on the database?
- How will the data be kept up to date and who is responsible for this?
- What data verification rules will be put in place to ensure quality and completeness?
- What analysis systems will the database support?
- Is there in-house expertise?
- Support offered
- Analysis systems support
- Maintenance costs
- Data capture, maintenance and enhancement
- Management issues – should the database be run in-house/out-of-house?

Profiling

Because of the range of information that is captured on customers, quite sophisticated profiles can be created. By linking a data base to services like Mosaic, the profile can be extended significantly. Simple profiling might be used to identify the best value customers, according to certain demographic or lifestyle indicators. This would be based on the value of past purchases, how often they purchased, and when they last purchased. This is known as recency, frequency and value analysis, or RFV analysis. It is also written as FRAC analysis (Frequency Recency Amount and Category). By matching this to other data, e.g. income, family status and postcode, people with similar profiles can be targeted.

Using the Database to Profile Customers

The Data Warehouse and Data Marts

There is an important difference between the database, data marts and data warehouses. In many ways they are different levels of the same thing – the range of data held on customers and marketing and other activities within an organization. A data mart is a collection of databases that may serve a particular purpose. These tend to be expensive to maintain as they duplicate information.

Data warehouses are created to form a single view of the 'truth' for the organization as a whole and consolidate data marts. The creation of data warehousing may involve a complex reorganization of business processes.

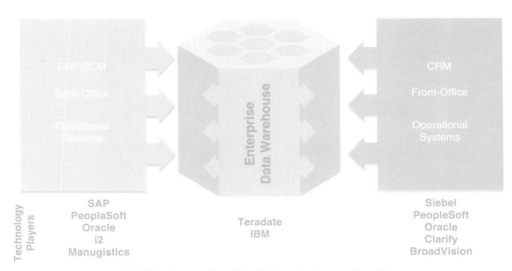

Data Warehouses Combine Datamarts. Source: Teradata

The development of the data warehouse may be an expensive task especially around the integration of different systems and platforms. However, the advantages are clear and the enabling of complex decisions, not just at the marketing level, is one clear benefit. As the warehouse becomes more established, the level of decision-making its supports becomes higher

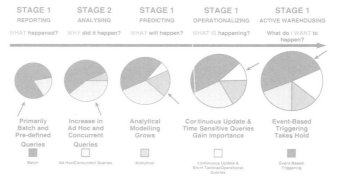

Figure 3.3 Information evolution in data warehousing
Source: Teradata

Data mining

- Data mining is the process of analyzing the database or the data warehouse to extract meaningful and actionable information. Antinou defines it as 'the process of extracting hidden and actionable information for large databases' (Antinou, T., 1997)

- Data mining software can help this process. It includes the process of statistical analysis of data or simple counts. It also includes a range of tools to help analyze the database. These are known as online analytical processing, or OLAP. OLAP tools allow for queries to be made of data, e.g. counts of the number of people of a certain age who bought a particular product. These tools allow the database to be interrogated

Other Analysis Techniques

Regression identifies the nature of a relationship. Regression analysis scores individuals according to their characteristics. For example, buyers of a certain product may have certain other characteristics. They may:

- Live in certain areas
- Have certain income levels
- Have a certain number of children

By applying this to all records and scoring those records, we can predict those with the highest scores have a greater tendency to buy.

Cluster analysis – Groups customers according to their general characteristics. This can be used to create segments from the database.

CHAID analysis – Is used to break down the customer base into segments based on certain key variables. It is used to target subgroups on the database more effectively.

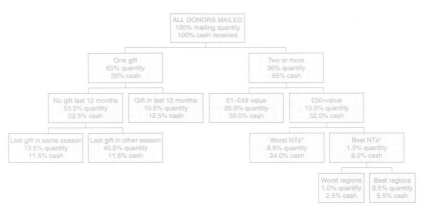

Figure 3.4 An example of CHAID analysis in fundraising
Source: The IDM (2005)

The analysis shows that the number of previous gifts would have been the best variable:

36 percent who sent 2 or more donations account for 65 percent of the money.

This model shows 88.5 percent of the cash could have been raised from just 60 percent of the mailing list.

10.5% Yields 12.5% cash

26.0% Yields 33% cash

10.0% Yields 32% cash

13.5% Yields 11% cash

60% Volume ¼ 88.5% cash

How Can the Data be Used? (I)

The data can be used in a number of ways. The case below presents an outline of how the Database works in Financial Services.

The financial services sector is a heavy-user of database analysis. Amongst others, a major bank has used their database in the following ways:

1. To manage the branch network
   (a) Identifying the most profitable branches
   (b) Staff appraisal, monitoring, reward and recognition
   (c) To identify staff training needs
   (d) To manage branch location.
2. To acquire new customers
   (a) Through profiling of good, existing customers and using this
   (b) To plan for the acquisition of new customers.
3. To increase profitability of existing customers
   (a) Reducing the cost of marketing

    (b) Improved targeting

    (c) Personalizing marketing communications

    (d) Reduce attrition.

4. Developing new products

5. Developing new market segments.

How Can the Data be Used? (II)

- Planning – Defining objectives, segmentation studies, targeting, campaign management costs analysis and return on investment
- Contacting customers – Which medium or combination of media is the most effective and efficient, at what time?
- Data processing – Counts and reports to aid planning
- Production – Production of lists and labels for address management; producing lists for follow up activities; merging letter copy and addresses
- Response handling – Recording responses to promotional mailings via unique tracking codes
- Lead processing – Tracking enquiries through 'to sale' and 'after sales'
- Campaign management – Customer paperwork and reports to help manage promotions
- Customer research – Information from questionnaires may be added to records to make the future planning process more effective
- Analysis – Pre-determined reports and other analysis

Marketing applications of the database can be summed up as:

- Finding
- Acquiring
- Keeping
- Cross-selling additional products
- Up-selling higher value products
- Prevent inactivity
- Renewing

Hints and Tips

- Thomas and Housden's book *Direct Marketing in Practice* contains a useful chapter on the database and its applications
- Technology has enabled the development of the database into a powerful tool for the management of customer information
- It is essential that any database is kept up-to-date through regular 'cleaning', or customer relationships can be damaged rather than enhanced
- Customer databases provide information on purchase behaviour, customer loyalty and customer response, but they only describe 'what' and not 'why'
- A data warehouse is a large database, storing transactional data and enabling insightful analysis
- Data mining selects, explores and models large amounts of data to uncover previously unknown relationships and patterns

- Marketing research should be transparent about database usage and should not be used to 'sell' to respondents
- Much marketing intelligence information can come from making better use of existing information. For instance, by carrying out database analysis on orders taken, it may be possible to understand where there are cross-sale and up-sale opportunities, or to understand what type of customers are the most profitable

Go to www.cimvirtualinstitute.com and www.marketingonline.co.uk for additional support and guidance

THE MARKETING RESEARCH PROCESS

Syllabus Reference: 3.2–3.6

After completing this unit you will:

- ■ Be able to identify the stages of a marketing research plan
- ■ Identify and brief a range of marketing research suppliers
- ■ Be able to construct a proposal document in response to a marketing research brief

Key definitions

- Primary research – Research carried out for the first time with participants
- Secondary research – Published research or research carried out for some other purpose
- Experimental research – Research measuring causality, or the changing of one variable to observe the effect on another, whilst other extraneous variables are kept constant
- Coding – The process of allocating codes to responses collected during fieldwork, facilitating analysis of data (MRS, 2003)
- Exploratory research – Research intended to develop initial ideas or insights and to provide direction for any further research
- Fieldwork – The collection of primary data from external sources by means of surveys, observation and experiment
- Longitudinal research – Data collection over time to examine trends
- Causal research – Research that examines whether one variable causes or determines the value of another variable
- Descriptive research – Research studies that describe what's happening in a market without potentially explaining why it is happening
- Observation research – A non-verbal means of obtaining primary data as an alternative or complement to questioning

There is a *gold standard* for all researchers and everyone interested in research wants to know the following:

- *Reliability* – the extent to which a study's findings can be replicated or reproduced by another inquirer using the same methods of data collection
- *Objectivity* – the extent to which findings are free from bias
- *Internal validity* – the degree to which findings correctly map the phenomenon in question
- *External validity* – the degree to which findings can be generalized to other settings similar to the one in which the study occurred

It is difficult to find definitive answers to these questions because it would often require expensive replica studies to test reliability and validity. The best that might be hoped for is that for those involved in commissioning, conducting and interpreting research do their best to design and conduct research studies that aspire to be as reliable, valid and objective as possible.

The Marketing Research Plan

1. Review the business situation
2. Define the marketing issue or problem
3. Carry out exploratory research
4. Previous research
5. Internal research
6. Redefine the problem

7. Brief issued
8. Agency selected
9. Research design
10. Desk research
11. Primary research
    - Qualitative
    - Quantitative

12. Pilot
13. Fieldwork
14. Data input coding and editing
15. Data analysis
16. Results
17. Findings and recommendations
18. Report/presentation
19. Decision

Review the Business Situation

Start the process with a review of the current business position. Restating the values and mission of the business, identifying markets served and a unique selling proposition helps to focus the research process on the broader goals of the business. It may help to state the marketing objectives of the business and summarize the current marketing plan, which should provide the underpinning for all activities.

- Marketing decisions need to be made in response to a constantly changing business environment and research may be needed to inform these decisions
- The review of the business environment is an ongoing process and research requirements may reflect the dynamic nature of this environment
- Environmental scanning may be the responsibility of the research department
- The business case needs to be established, as resources within the marketing function are always under pressure. The research proposed needs to be fully informed by the business situation and an assessment of relative costs and benefits

Defining the Issues or Problem

Poor problem definition can lead to expensive and unnecessary work being carried out. Exploratory research should clarify the research problem. It is largely informal and may involve a range of techniques. It should involve discussions with those who are involved with the problem and its solution. The aim is to inform the process and to become 'immersed' in the problem and its potential solutions. An understanding of the commercial constraints of carrying out research needs to be worked out. It is incumbent on the person making the business case to clarify the assumptions that they are making and explaining the rationale that will lead to increased sales. This information is needed for critical internal scrutiny.

Internal Research

This should be reviewed to see if the problem has been dealt with elsewhere. It may be that the solution lies in the work that has been done in other departments. Internal research will involve the use of the MkIS and the database. It may be that the problem can be solved at this stage.

Redefine the Problem

The output of this stage is a clear statement of the research problem that is agreed by all parties. After this, a brief can be written.

Research Design

Wilson identifies three types of marketing research. These are:

1. Exploratory
2. Conclusive – descriptive research
3. Conclusive – causal research

$what \begin{Bmatrix} who \\ what \\ where \\ when \end{Bmatrix} happening \ but \ NOT \ why.$

Whilst these are not mutually exclusive, they represent a continuum, from purely descriptive to the causal.

Desk Research

Desk or secondary research is information that has already been gathered for some other purpose. It is usually accessible from a desk via the Intranet, online, or in hard copy.

Primary Research

Primary research is 'new to the world research'. It uses methods such as telephone research, face-to-face interviews, or online research.

Quantitative Research

Quantitative research provides answers to the questions 'who' and 'how many', rather than the depth of insight as to 'why'. It uses a structured approach to problem-solving, using a sample of the population to make statistically based assumptions about the behaviour of the population as a whole. Quantitative research is usually gathered and recorded via a questionnaire. It can be delivered via a number of different media, including face-to-face, telephone, mail, or online.

The Pilot

Research should be piloted or tested to check that the data collection methods are sound. Pilots will help with the structure and sequencing of questions and may identify areas of questioning that have not been considered.

Fieldwork

Fieldwork covers the collection of observational, quantitative and qualitative data. The administration of a major study may involve serious logistical considerations. The management of fieldwork is often given to specialist field managers or fieldwork agencies. The process is important, as failure to adhere to the correct methodology at this stage may compromise the entire project.

Data input, coding and editing – Data gathered from respondents must be recorded and edited to produce a data set that can be analyzed. In qualitative work, this may be transcripts of interviews. In quantitative work, data can be input straight into the computer via:

- Computer-aided telephone interviewing (CATI)
- Computer-aided personal interviewing (CAPI)
- Computer-aided web interviewing (CAWI)

Data analysis – Data is analyzed via the computer to produce a range of results.

Results, findings and recommendations – Results should be presented clearly in a way that focuses on the problem to be solved. They should be presented in a way that is accessible to the audience and that clearly presents the solution to the problem posed.

Report/presentation – Presentation of the results will usually be in the form of a written report and this may be supported by an oral presentation. The data will need to be presented, but this should be in the appendices. The body of the report remains solutions-focused.

Decision – The output should be marketing decisions that are made at reduced risk and a feedback loop should exist to the business situation.

The Marketing Research Brief

- The briefing document is perhaps the most important stage of the research process
- A tight brief is vital to the management of the marketing research process. It provides a focus for discussion and a guiding hand through the project
- Some research briefs are given on one side of an A4 page. This may be sufficient but may be adequate for complex multifaceted research tasks
- The best marketing solutions come through cooperation and active involvement.
- The development of the brief should be a team activity

Short Listing

Once the brief is written and agreed, it should be sent to a short list of agencies. The short list generally should be no longer than four. Occasionally, more than four agencies are asked to pitch. It is courteous to let the agencies know how many other companies they are up against. Clients should not normally invite more than four agencies to tender in writing for a project. Unless paid for by the client, a specification for a project drawn-up by one research agency is the property of that agency and may not be passed on to another agency without the permission of the originating research agency.

The proposal – The proposal should be presented in a written format and on time. A formal presentation may accompany it.

Identification data
   Key contact details, title and data.
Situation analysis
   An outline of the current business position.
Research objectives
   A clear statement of the purpose of the research.
Methodology and rationale
   Crouch and Housden (Crouch, S. and Housden, M., 2003) suggest that the following
   type of questions should be answered:
   * Why use the sample selection procedure indicated?
   * Why use the size of sample indicated?
   * Why the personal interview technique rather than group discussion?
   * Why a 20-minute questionnaire and not a 30-minute questionnaire?
   * Why are open-ended questions requiring expensive coding and analysis being included
     in a large-scale quantitative survey?
   * Why is a written report or verbal presentation included, or why not?
   * Why the timetable indicated?
   * Why is the cost indicated?

Contd.

Sample
   A precise definition of the sample to be selected and a justification of this.
Fieldwork
   What data collection methods are proposed?
Questionnaire/topic guide
   It is unreasonable to expect a final questionnaire but an indication of what the agency
   expects to see in the questionnaire should be provided.
Data handling and processing
   How will data be captured, edited, coded and analyzed? What tables will be provided?
   How will the data be presented?
Reporting
   What is included in the cost?

Contd.

Timetable

A full detailed timetable of research activity and key milestones.

Costs

What is included? Is VAT included? How long is the quote valid? Terms of business and payment schedule.

CVs of key staff

Are people who are presenting the people you will be dealing with? What is their experience? What professional memberships do they have?

Supporting evidence

Is the agency a member of professional bodies? Are references provided?

Contract details: the proposal will generally form the contract on acceptance.

Selecting the Agency

Wilson (2003) identifies a checklist of seven points:

1. The agency's ability to understand the brief and translate it into a comprehensive proposal
2. The compatibility of agency and client teams. Can we work with them?
3. The evidence of innovation in the proposal. Has the agency added value?
4. Evidence of understanding of the market and the problem facing the organization
5. Sound methodology
6. Meeting budget and time scales
7. Relevant experience

Managing the Agency Relationship

(Baker, S. and Mouncey, P., 2003)

- Get involved with the marketing team
- Anticipate research opportunities
- Develop research tools that relate to the commercial issues the company and its clients face
- Deliver research more effectively and more efficiently
- Investigate opportunities to deliver research 'online'
- Encourage informal contact with users
- 'Educate' senior management about the value of research to the business
- Be intellectually attuned to your key clients' needs

International Research

Proctor (2003) suggests four different approaches to carrying out international research

- Using own staff or importing agents – problems here may be due to lack of impartiality and lack of skills
- Using overseas agencies – selection may be difficult, but they should possess knowledge of their home markets
- Using a UK-based firm supported by locally based researchers – this offers few advantages over the above
- Using a consortium of agencies – problems here include variability between agencies

Recruiting international agencies should be straightforward, but there are a range of additional complexities involved. For example, language and cultural differences need to be recognized and built into research design.

In-house or out-of-house research ?

In-house has a range of advantages:

- Control of the research process rests with those who commissioned the work
- Awareness of the market or sector dynamics
- Knowledge of both methodology and results resides within the organization – cumulative knowledge
- Costs – it may be cheaper to manage the tasks in-house
- Timing – it may be quicker to produce results

Disadvantages include:

- Lack of skills or methodological expertise
- Inability to provide true national or international coverage
- Bias in terms of interpreting the result from a predetermined point of view

Advantages of using an agency include

- Penalty clauses in contracts can protect the commissioning party
- MRS code of conduct or other industry quality control standards will ensure the integrity of data
- There is no political element to the research

Disadvantages

- Conflict of interest with other clients
- Lack of industry expertise
- Allocation of junior staff to smaller projects

Evaluating Existing Research

A scheme for judging research quality

1. **What were the objectives of the research?**
   Are they appropriate to the problem to which the finding are now to be applied?

2. **What method was used to collect the information?**
   Is it appropriate to the information needed?

3. **Who was asked the questions?**
   Is the sample definition appropriate?

4. **How many people were asked?**
   Is the sample size adequate?

5. **What were the actual questions?**
   Check the copy of the questionnaire in the technical appendix. Do they seem to be good questions – well framed and appropriate to the objectives?

6. **Who did the fieldwork?**
   Is there a basis for judging the quality of the fieldwork? Were professional interviewers used? What checking procedure were used?

Contd

7. **When was the field carried out?**
   Was the timing sufficiently recent for the results still to hold? Was the time of year/time of day appropriate?

8. **Are the tabulations comprehensible?**
   Are they legible, with clear headings, and indexed?

9. **Would further cross-tabulations produce useful information?**
   Are these possible?

10. **Is the report in a logical order and readable?**
    Does it make sense?

11. **Is there a meaningful summary?**
    Is it easy to grasp the main points being made?

12. **Are there conclusions? (if appropriate)**
    Are they supported by the data?

13. **Did the research meet its objectives, and if not, why not?**
    Does this invalidate the research?

A Scheme for Judging Research Quality. Source: Crouch and Housden 2003

Hints and Tips

- The market research industry is made up of full service agencies, specialist service agencies, field agencies, data analysis services and independent consultants
- The industry is self-regulated by professional bodies such as the Market Research Society
- External suppliers can be useful as they may be more objective, have specialist skills, specialist facilities and experience in the specific market/topic
- Base selection on experience, technical expertise, resources, reputation, communication skills and length of time in industry
- The research proposal is the most important of the whole research project. The proposal is based on the brief given and provides a template and contract for the project
- The process of defining the initial research problem can be helped by internal and exploratory research. The use of research should be justified, where possible, by examining the cost of making a poor marketing decision, compared to the anticipated profit from making a better marketing decision
- Start with the cheapest sources of information; that is, secondary or desk research. If this does not produce the required information, then primary research should be considered
- Qualitative work should precede and inform the development and use of quantitative methods

Go to www.cimvirtualinstitute.com and www.marketingonline.co.uk for additional support and guidance

USING SECONDARY RESEARCH

Unit 5

Syllabus Reference: 4.1, 4.2

On completing this unit you will be able:

- To define secondary marketing research
- To explain types of secondary data
- To understand where to find secondary data
- To understand the limitations and strengths of secondary research
- To look for data online
- To understand the applications of secondary research

Key definitions

- External data – Data that is held by external organizations
- Internet – A network of computers
- World Wide Web – An Internet protocol supervised by the world wide web consortium at www.w3.org
- Intranet – A closed private company network based on web technology
- Extranet – A process that shares information from internal sources with selected external organizations
- Search engines – Internet-based tools for searching for Uniform Resource Location (URL) or web addresses
- Newsgroups – Web-based bulletin board services
- Chat rooms – Locations on the Internet enabling web-based text or video-based real time interaction
- ISP – Internet service provider

Crouch and Housden (Crouch, S. and Housden, M., 2003) define secondary desk research as 'data that has already been published by someone else, at some other time period, usually for some other reason than the present researcher has in mind. The researcher is therefore a secondary user of already existing data which can be obtained and worked on at a desk'.

The Strengths and Weaknesses of Secondary Data

Strengths

- It is cheap or free of charge. Costs vary, but very often a full report on markets or market sectors can be put together very quickly and cheaply
- It may provide an answer to the problem – this will save enormous time and effort
- It can guide or provide direction for primary work
- It can suggest methodologies for data collection
- It can indicate problems with particular methodologies
- It can provide historic or comparative data to enable longitudinal studies

Weaknesses

- It is not related to the research question and the temptation may be to force the data to fit the question
- It may not be directly comparable. This is particularly the case in international markets where markets may be defined differently
- Data may be incomplete
- It may not be available. It may be that there are certain markets that are not adequately covered
- The data may have been gathered for a particular purpose. Production statistics in certain markets are unreliable. Data may be presented to portray a company or government in a more favourable light
- Data for international markets may be more expensive and unreliable
- Data for international markets may be in a foreign language. Translating costs in business markets are expensive
- Time series data may be interrupted by definition changes, e.g. in the way inflation is calculated

Both Wilson (2003) and Crouch and Housden (2003) have significant resources outlined in the relevant chapters.

Evaluating Secondary Data

When looking at published research reports, the user should ask the following questions:

- Who published the study? Was it a national government? Was it a trade association?
- What is the nature of the organization? Is the publisher of the data the same as the organization that collected the data?
- For what purpose? Is the study designed to sell a service? Is it designed to counter negative publicity? Is it designed to generate publicity?
- When was the data gathered? Is it relevant?
- How was the data collected? Was the data capture mechanism reliable? Was it a self-selecting sample?
- Who collected the data? Are they independent? Are they trained? Are they members of a professional body? What sample was used?
- How reliable is the data?
- Is raw data presented?
- Can I replicate the study? Is the methodology included? Can I test the data for accuracy?
- Is the data comparable?

Sources of Secondary Data

The emergence of the Internet as a key information consolidator and provider has increased the availability of information to the desk researcher. It has increased access to previously remote information, for example, data held in libraries overseas and it has increased the ability to distribute this information.

Searching Online

Successful online searching will be achieved if the search terms are carefully defined. Careful phrasing of the search term and creative use of Boolean operators can help.

Boolean operators are usually found in the advance search section in the search engine or directory. Boolean logic operators help the browser search the web. The simplest of these are the words 'and' or 'þ', 'not' or '–' and 'or'. Others may allow the use of what are known as proximity operators, such as 'followed by' or 'near'. These can help refine search terms and produce more relevant results.

The use of Google's advance search feature can reduce the number of results for any search term to far more manageable and relevant numbers. There are directories of search engines at www.searchability.com and www.virtualfreesites.com.

Newsgroups, Blogs and Discussion Forums

Newsgroups exist for almost every topic including marketing research. Newsgroups can be useful sources of information and also for establishing opinions on products and services. Some companies monitor newsgroups for research purposes and some seed newsgroups with product information and recommendations. This is a dubious practice if it is not done transparently and if uncovered can lead to the user being barred from the service.

Most search engines allow groups to be searched for. Try www.groups.google.com.

Blogs can be very useful sources of information and there are significant resources available on research and marketing. Search via http://blogsearch.google.com, to find relevant content.

Hints and Tips

- Both Wilson (Wilson, A., 2003) and Crouch and Housden (Crouch, S. and Housden, M., 2003) have significant resources outlined in the relevant chapters. You should scan these chapters and add relevant websites to your list of favourites

- Secondary data is information that has been previously gathered for some purpose other than the current project. It helps to clarify the requirements, enables more insightful interpretation of primary data, provides comparative data, and provides information that cannot be obtained through primary research

- Secondary data is faster and less expensive to collect – the Internet has improved this still further, but its limitations include availability, applicability, accuracy and comparability and its use should be evaluated before going ahead

Go to www.cimvirtualinstitute.com and www.marketingonline.co.uk for additional support and guidance

OBSERVATION RESEARCH

After completing this unit you will be able to:

- Define observational research
- Understand the methods of observational research
- Understand and define the role of audits in marketing research
- Understand the application of mystery shopping techniques
- Identify online observation techniques
- Outline the ethical issues in observational research

Key definition

- Observation – A non-verbal means of obtaining primary data as an alternative or complement to questioning (MRS, 2003)
- Panels – A permanent representative sample, maintained by a market research agency, from which information is obtained on more than one occasion, either for continuous research or for ad hoc projects (MRS, 2003)

Contd.

- Audit – The measurement of product volume and value through the distribution network. Audit may be wholesale, retail or consumer
- Mystery shopping – The use of individuals trained to observe, experience and measure the customer service process, by acting as a prospective customer and undertaking a series of predetermined tasks (MRS, 1997)
- Peoplemeter – The mechanical device used by BARB to collect data on TV audiences in the UK
- EPOS – Electronic Point Of Sale equipment
- Cookies – A file stored on your hard drive, used to identify your computer and other information, including preferences to another remote computer
- Ethnographic research – Observation involving total immersion in the life of the subject

Definitions of observation research

The MRS defines observation as 'A non-verbal means of obtaining primary data as an alternative or complement to questioning' (MRS, 2003). Wilson defines it as 'a data gathering approach where information on the behaviour of people, objects and organizations is collected without any questions being asked of the participant' (Wilson, A., 2003).

Observation strengths

- It is not dependent on the respondent's memory. It records exactly what has happened, not what the respondent believes has happened

- The potential for bias in research may be reduced, as the researcher is the witness of behaviour rather than actively asking for information – the way an interviewer asks for information can influence responses

- Mechanical recording of observed behaviour may reduce the incidence of reporting errors

- Observation does not rely on the verbal skills of a respondent to describe the behaviour

- Observation measures what has happened, not what respondents say that they will do in a certain situation.

- Observation can counter the high refusal rates in some markets

- Observation can be used to monitor behaviour preceding an action, e.g. picking up and looking at competing products before making a final decision

- Observation does not interfere with the respondents' day-to-day life. It is their activity that is of interest. They do not have to fill in diaries or complete questionnaires

Disadvantages

- Observation does not measure the reasons for certain behaviour. It cannot uncover motivation or attitudes
- Observation cannot measure the likelihood of repeat behaviour
- Only public behaviour can be assessed. Private behaviour is very difficult to research in this way, although efforts have been made to manage this process

Categories of observation research

Wilson (2003) identifies five different categories of observation research. These are:

1. Natural versus contrived
2. Visible versus hidden
3. Structured versus unstructured
4. Mechanized versus human
5. Participant versus non-participant

Natural	Contrived
Rather like David Attenborough and mountain gorillas, customers are observed in their natural state	The researcher sets up an observation situation
Respondents may be observed going around a supermarket, browsing a website and so on	This may be a supermarket fixture set up in a room or children playing with new toys with the researcher present
They are not aware that they are being observed	Customers are aware that they are being observed
Visible	**Hidden**
Customers are aware that observation is taking place because they can see the recording equipment	Respondents know that they are being observed but cannot see the observer or recording equipment
Structured	**Unstructured**
Observers keep a tally or count of certain behaviours	Observers record or make notes on all aspects of the observed behaviour
Mechanical	**Human**
The installation of equipment to measure behaviour	More appropriate for complex behaviour involving multiple interactions
Participant	**Non-participant**
The observer participates in the observed behaviour, for example, in mystery shopping	The behaviour is observed remotely

Observation methodologies

There are a range of observational techniques that are used throughout the research industry.

Audits and scanner-based observation

An audit measures product movement and consumption through the value chain. There are three types of audit – wholesale, retail and home. The use of Electronic Point Of Sale (EPOS) and hand-held scanning devices has changed this sector of the market significantly over the last 10 years.

Audits have been in place for some time, but the process of carrying them out was far more time consuming than it is today. The use of EPOS technology has significantly reduced the amount of time taken to produce results. Audit data can produce a huge range of analysis, and the services of AC Neilsen and TN Sofres provide the raw material for the marketing management of the retail and grocery marketing sector. The data includes:

- Market share
- Brand share
- Brand loyalty
- Category loyalty
- Retail sector analysis
- Retail share
- Retail price checks
- Average basket
- Sales promotion responses, etc.

Media measurement

The measurement of media is a key element of observation research. The most important is the **Broadcaster's Audience Research Board (BARB)**, which provides the measurement service for television viewing in the UK. Other media are audited in different ways – some are based on observation, some on other research methods.

Other Observation Techniques

Ethnography

Ethnography is a research technique that has been used in the social sciences for some time and is increasingly used in marketing. The research may look at family interaction with a product or brand and may be looking for depth of insight to inform market positioning.   *football – hooliganism*

Mechanical observation

A range of mechanical observation techniques are used in observation research which include psychogalvanometers. This measures the respondents' reaction to a message. It uses the same techniques as a lie detector, measuring the electrical resistance of the skin. The amount of sweat on the skin increases during arousal and it is this that is measured. It is most often used for pre-testing advertising and copy.

Pupilmeters

Pupilmeters measure the same responses through a measurement of pupil dilation.

Eye cameras

Eye cameras are used to track the movement of the eye around an object, maybe a piece of creative or a retail fixture. This method has been used on websites' research to explore the navigation of sites and may be combined with a mechanical record of key strokes or mouse movement.

Tachistoscopes

Reveal the test material in microsecond bursts. The respondents' ability to recall detail is measured. It is believed to predict advertising effectiveness amongst other uses.

Mystery shopping

The use of individuals trained to observe, experience and measure the customer service process, by acting as a prospective customer and undertaking a series of pre-determined tasks (MRS, 1997). This may be done by companies assessing the activities of competitors in the market, or by companies assessing the performance of their own sales staff.

Wilson (Wilson, A., 2003) identifies three main purposes for mystery shopping:

1. To act as a diagnostic tool, identifying failings and weak points in service delivery
2. To encourage and reward staff
3. To assess competitors

Online observation

The use of cookies allows a website owner to identify repeat visits. A cookie is a text file placed on the browser's computer that allows the browser's computer to be identified on subsequent visits. A cookie may contain the computer's address or the details of a customer registration. This means that, when the customer logs on, a personalized greeting can be made or passwords provided. Most online retailers use this system, e.g. Amazon will drive content to particular customers, based on their previous behaviour. Browser behaviour through the site can also be captured and used.

Ethics in observation research

There are clearly significant ethical considerations in the use of observation research. The basic rule is that, if observation is to take place in a situation in which behaviour could not usually be observed, then permission should be asked.

International issues

The use of observation is appropriate in all markets. Indeed, in some international markets it may be the preferred method. In addition to the usual international caveats of cost, comparability and availability of resources, for example CCTV, we have to add the problem of interpretation.

The interpretation of body language, signs (semiotics) and non-verbal behaviour is culturally determined. For example. in certain African countries it is not unusual for men to hold hands as they are walking together. In other markets, colours may mean something very different from the UK. In China, red means good luck while in other countries it means danger. In some other markets, green is the colour for danger. In the UK, white is the colour representing purity and is worn by brides at their weddings. In Japan, white is the colour of mourning, and in Brazil, purple is the colour of mourning.

As well as being self aware of the potential for bias, where possible, a researcher should also use local agencies who can help to interpret phenomena from an indigenous cultural perspective.

Hints and Tips

- ■ Observation measures behaviour, not reasons for the behaviour
- ■ Mystery shopping measures service delivery, often retail, researchers work to a brief as a customer, aims to be objective and collect facts, and more than one visit may be required
- ■ Observation can be carried out mechanically through scanners, electronic TV viewing meters, Internet cookies, and security or CCTV cameras
- ■ There are ethical issues that arise in observation research and 'informed consent' should be the principle to guide the observation of behaviour
- ■ Make sure you are aware of the strengths and weaknesses of different approaches and for what purposes they are most appropriate
- ■ Collect actual examples of how observation research is used

Go to www.cimvirtualinstitute.com and www.marketingonline.co.uk for additional support and guidance

QUALITATIVE RESEARCH

Syllabus Reference: 4.4–4.6

After completing this unit you will be able to:

- Define qualitative data
- Identify and apply methods for collecting qualitative data
- Understand the process of analyzing qualitative data
- Understand the techniques of online qualitative research
- Understand how to use qualitative research to inform marketing decision-making

Key definitions

- Projective techniques – A form of disguised questioning that encourages participants to attribute their feelings, beliefs or motivations. Examples of projective techniques are word association, sentence completion and thematic apperception tests (ESOMAR, 2003)
- Moderator – An individual who facilitates but does not influence a group discussion

Contd.

- One-way window – A device used to allow researchers to view respondents without themselves being seen
- Depth interviews – A variety of data collection techniques, mainly for qualitative research, undertaken with individual respondents rather than groups (MRS, 2003)
- Topic or discussion guide – An outline of the structure, themes and timing of a focus group or depth interview
- Content analysis software – Computer software that helps with the textual analysis of qualitative research
- Brand personality tests – Asks respondents to describe a brand as a person

Qualitative research accounts for between 10 and 15 percent of total research expenditure in the UK. It is growing in importance as marketing professionals recognize its role in providing depth of understanding about customers and their behaviour. Wilson (2003) defines qualitative research as 'Research that is undertaken using an unstructured research approach, with a small number of carefully selected individuals, to produce non-quantifiable insights into behaviour motivations and attitudes'.

What are the essential characteristics of qualitative research?

- It is unquantifiable and is not representative of larger populations
- Data collection techniques are unstructured
- It involves small samples of individuals or groups of people
- It seeks to reveal opinions, motivations and attitudes
- It is about insight and depth of understanding
- It is subject to a high degree of interpretation by skilled researchers
- It often precedes quantitative work but can be independent of it (Figure 7.1)
- It can inform the nature of quantitative research

Comparative element	Qualitative research	Quantitative research
Type of questions	Probing	Non-probing
Sample size	Small	Large
Information per respondent	Much	Varies
Management	Special skills	Fewer skills
Type of analysis	Subjective	Statistical
Ease of replication	Difficult	Easy
Type of research	Exploratory	Descriptive or casual
Research training needed	Psychology	Statistics
	Sociology	Decision models
	Consumer Behaviour	Computer programming
	Marketing	Marketing
Hardware needed	Tape recorders	Computers
	Projection devices	PDA

Figure 7.1 Key differences between qualitative and quantitative work
Source: AMR (2003)

Data Collection Techniques in Qualitative Research

Focus groups or group discussions

The MRS defines group discussions or focus groups as 'A number of respondents gathered together to generate ideas through the discussion of, and reaction to, specific stimuli. Under the steerage of a moderator, focus groups are often used in exploratory work or when the subject matter involves social activities, habits and status' (MRS, 2003).

- Focus groups are generally made up of around 6–12 respondents. The most common number is 8. A lower number may be used when a particularly specialist topic is being discussed

- They are run and managed by a moderator, who will control the group, keeping the discussion on track and probing for further information when needed

- Groups will normally last between 45 minutes and 2 hours. Discussions are generally tape recorded or videographed

- Groups usually occur at the beginning of a research project, as they can provide very useful information to explore through other methods. The groups may be observed remotely and agencies offer clients the chance to view groups set up in special rooms, where the client can observe the group through a one-way window

Moderators should be:

- Highly qualified and experienced in research and managing groups
- Business and marketing aware. They need to be able to translate respondents' feelings into business advantage for their clients
- Strong communicators, able to relate to a range of people
- Hard to place regionally in terms of socioeconomic class
- Socially able, relaxed and friendly, but strong enough to control a room of animated, or, conversely, disinterested respondents
- Flexible and quick-thinking, with the ability to respond to the unexpected

Stimulus material

Stimulus material may include a range of physical objects which respondents can use to express their views non-verbally. These may include:

- Creative samples: Proofs, animated outlines of TV commercials, concept or storyboards, mail copy
- Mocked-up product packs
- Product samples

The topic or discussion guide

A discussion guide is designed as an aide memoire, to guide the moderator through the task of moderating a group of people. It is a route map for the group interview that outlines a timetable and highlights key stages in the process. It is not a list of questions. Wilson suggests that the guide breaks the group into three distinct phases:

1. Introduction
   a. Objectives
   b. Personal introductions
   c. Agenda
2. Discursive phase
   a. Topic areas
   b. Stimulus material
3. Summarizing phase
   a. Summarizing discussion
   b. Closing
   c. Administration

Depth interviews

This describes a variety of data collection techniques for qualitative research, undertaken with individual respondents rather than groups. Usually, in a study that involves depth interviews, 10–14 interviews will be carried out, depending on the nature of the sample. Depth interviews cost between £400 and £700 per interview.

Advantages:

- They are conducted face to face, and body language can be interpreted
- Proximity may encourage respondents to reveal more than in a remote interview
- The respondent is the centre of attention and can be probed at length to explore issues that the researcher feels are important. This is the 'annoying child' syndrome, with the researcher asking 'why' (but more subtly) until the issue is explored adequately
- Group dynamics may prevent individuals expressing themselves, particularly over areas that are sensitive, like income
- Recruitment tends to be easier
- The logistics are easier, no special rooms are needed
- They reveal depth of understanding
- They are flexible. The line of questioning may evolve within the interview and between interviews
- They can involve a range of techniques

Projective techniques

Projective techniques are designed to allow respondents to 'attribute their feelings, beliefs or motivations to another person, object or situation' (ESOMAR, 2003).

Advantages:

■ They are engaging for respondents, are usually fun to do, and get respondents motivated

■ They provide richer insight than conventional questioning: in the right hands the analysis can be extremely revealing

■ They can create excellent ideas for further exploration

The disadvantage is that they can be hard to interpret.

Sentence completion
Story completion
Word association
Cartoon completion
Mood boards
Brand personality

Brand mapping

These are also known as perceptual maps. Respondents are asked to identify key attributes or dimensions of a product sector and then position brands against those relative to the competition. This can be useful in identifying positioning and segmentation criteria and gaps in the market place. The alcopops sector was developed from this type of work. Consumers identified the fact that, as children, they drank fizzy, sweet, non-alcoholic drinks and as adults they drink flat, bitter or dry, alcoholic drinks. Alcopops filled the gap for sweet fizzy alcoholic drinks.

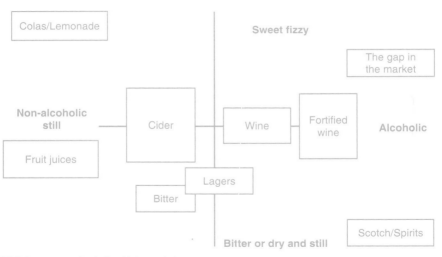

Figure 7.2 Category mapping in the drinks market

Online Qualitative Research

This includes depth interviews and focus groups. Focus groups use chat room technology to manage the interaction. People interact using their computers to talk to each other. Online bulletin boards are used to post messages and a group of people exchange information about a specific topic. Noticeboards are used to post messages and a group of people exchange information about a specific topic. Respondents are often recruited by e-mail and agree to participate at a certain time, at a certain URL. Each member is able to read the responses of other members and respond to their comments as if in a group situation. Depth interviewees are recruited in the same way but the communication takes place simply between the respondent and the interviewer.

The Web is not the ideal medium to deliver this type of research

- It is often hard to recruit suitable respondents
- Technical knowledge is required to participate and a common technical platform is required
- There are issues over the reliability of the Internet connection, and diverse browsers and so on
- Respondents may view screens at different speeds, in different frame sizes and so on
- Interaction is limited and body language cannot be seen although the use of web cams may help this
- It is hard to interpret sarcastic comments other than through the use of emoticons
- It is hard to maintain attention for long periods
- It is a less creative environment for respondents
- It is hard to moderate the contribution of all respondents
- It is hard to establish who exactly is sitting at the terminal

Advantages include:

- Bringing geographically dispersed samples together
- Online depth interviews have similar disadvantages but depth interviews online are hard to sustain for more than 10 minutes

- There are some advantages especially in b2b markets where the use of online techniques may fit more easily with the respondents' work practices

Analysis of Qualitative Data

The starting point is to organize the data, which is contained on tape. These tapes should always be kept. The analysis should enable the broad themes discussed during the research to be explored

Organizing the Data

Wilson (Wilson, A., 2003) suggests four methods for data organization:

- Tabular–In which data is organized according to certain characteristics or themes. The content from the groups or interviews is then divided into these areas. This can be done on spreadsheets or within word processing packages
- Cut and paste–Material is physically cut from transcript and pasted into separate thematic sections
- Spider diagrams or mind maps–Places the material at the centre of a diagram with responses emanating from the centre
- Annotation–The researcher annotates the transcript to bring together common themes

Hints and Tips

- Ideas that qualitative research methods are 'second' best approach rest in large part because of the predominance of the 'scientific' model of social research. The central values of the latter approach are objectivity and generalizability

- In contrast, qualitative approaches emphasize the importance of getting close to the subject. This is because one of the purposes of qualitative approaches is to try to depict the participant's views. Because of the time and costs involved in such work, qualitative designs do not generally draw samples from large-scale data sets. Ideas of 'second' best also rest on the stereotypes that arise when quantitative and qualitative approaches are compared in this way

- In some ways the concerns that arise about a qualitative/quantitative divide can be resolved by giving greater attention to how these approaches can be combined

- The CAQDAS Networking Project was set up, in conjunction with ESRC, to disseminate an understanding of the practical skills needed to use software to facilitate qualitative data analysis and to encourage debate about issues raised by the use of such software. http://caqdas.soc.surrey.ac.uk/

- The most important issue regarding types of research is 'fitness for purpose', i.e. will the research approach yield the data that is needed and help to ensure that the research objectives are achieved

Go to www.cimvirtualinstitute.com and www.marketingonline.co.uk for additional support and guidance

QUANTITATIVE DATA

Syllabus Reference: 4.4–4.6

After completing this unit you will be able to:

- Define quantitative data
- Understand the methods for collecting quantitative data
- Identify online methods for online quantitative data capture
- Define and describe the use of CAPI, CATI and CAWI
- Explore the range of applications enabled by quantitative research

Key definitions

- CAPI – Computer Aided Personal interviewing
- CAWI – Computer Aided Web interviewing
- CATI – Computer Aided Telephone interviewing
- Omnibus surveys – 'A survey covering a number of topics, usually for different clients. The samples tend to be nationally representative and composed of types of people for which there is a general demand. Clients are charged by the market research agency on the basis of the questionnaire space or the number of questions required' (MRS, 2003)

What is quantitative data?

Wilson identifies five key characteristics of quantitative data:

- Data gathering is more structured
- Research involves larger samples than qualitative research
- The data gathered can provide answers that will quantify the incidence of particular behaviour motivations and attitudes in the population under consideration
- Studies can be more easily replicated and direct comparisons can be made between studies
- Analysis is statistical in nature and will usually be done with the help of computer software

Survey methods

Surveys are defined by the MRS as 'The systematic collection, analysis and interpretation of information about some aspect of study. In market research, the term is applied particularly to the collection of information by means of sampling and interviews with the selected individuals' (MRS, 2003).

Face-to-face interviews

These are interviews that are carried out with respondents in face-to-face contact with the interviewer; results are recorded on paper or digitally on a Personal Digital Assistant, palmtop or laptop computer. These can be distinguished from interviewer-administered surveys that are carried out remotely via the telephone or a 'help me' button on a web page.

Face-to-face data collection: Advantages

- There is greater acceptance of the validity of the research if an interviewer can introduce the reasons for the research and show professional membership cards

- The interview process is more efficient as non-eligible respondents can be screened out more effectively

- They improve response rates as the interviewer can answer questions or help with any difficulty in completing the questionnaire

- Personal contact creates a sense of obligation and this can be useful with long surveys. This can reduce the incidence of incomplete or unfinished interviews

- Complexity can be introduced into the survey – for example, the use of show cards or other stimuli material is more easily managed

■ Empathy and encouragement can enable deeper consideration of the questions and ensure accuracy of some claims – for example, gender and age

Face-to-face Disadvantages

■ Costs particularly in b2b research may be high, but this must be offset against a higher response rate.
■ It can take a considerable amount of time to complete a survey
■ Interviewers may be demotivated and may take short cuts to ensure that their quota of completed surveys is made
■ Interview bias is a problem. Bias may affect:
  – Who is interviewed
  – The way questions are asked
  – The way an interviewer responds verbally and visually to an answer
  – The way an answer is recorded
■ Safety of interviewing staff may be an issue in some areas
■ The training and control of field staff is important and adds to costs
■ A dispersed sample geographically, for example regional store mangers, is clearly difficult to administer in this way and other data collection methods might need to be considered

In-home or doorstep interviews

These are interviews carried out at the home of the respondent. These may be important if the sample is determined by post code or type of dwelling. They have the advantage of putting the respondent at their ease but are generally hard to manage.

Street interviews

These are perhaps the most visible forms of marketing research. Street interviewing has a number of advantages:

- They are less expensive than home interviews
- They allow respondents who conform to quota specifications to be identified and approached – e.g. women with children or older men

Disadvantages include:

- Some shopping centres charge a fee or do not allow researchers to interview customers
- Respondents are unlikely to stop in the open air if it is raining
- Interviews need to be as short as possible
- There are many distractions to the respondent – e.g. children or friends who are impatient

Telephone

- Acceptance of it as a means of communication
- UK is largest user of call centres in Europe
- Mobile phones and Internet enable research using a range of methods

Advantages:

- At around £10–£20 per interview cost is lower than face-to-face. Larger surveys can be administered via a call centre at around £5 per call. Possible to run a research programme using voice recognition software
- Control is much easier. Software enables calls to be recorded or monitored
- Bias due to non-verbal influence is removed and verbal influence can be controlled through the monitoring process
- Good for geographically dispersed samples saving travel costs and time
- Convenient for interviewer and respondent. Calls may be made that allow the interviewer to call back at a convenient time to deliver the interview
- Third generation mobile phones, mobile Internet and SMS text messaging, have extended the capability of the phone as a medium for data capture

Disadvantages:

- Lower response rates than face-to-face interviews
- Respondents find it easier to say 'no' on the telephone
- Research design is restricted. The use of stimuli is limited and length of interview is shorter than face-to-face interviews, in order to maintain the interest of the respondent
- Some social classes have a greater preponderance of ex-directory numbers
- Access to mobile telephone numbers may be difficult to obtain
- The use of cold calling by certain market sectors has created a problem for market researchers

CAPI

Computer Assisted Personal Interviewing is conducted face-to-face, usually employing Personal Digital Assistants (PDAs) and, if these are connected to a mobile telephone network, results can be uploaded immediately.

Advantages:

- Data entry is much simpler

- There is no print production, so it is cheaper

- The computer can check for inconsistent replies – for example, a respondent has said that he is a non-smoker and later tells an interviewer he smokes on average three cigarettes a week

- Telephone is one of the fastest growing media to collect data. We looked at the reasons for this

  - Changing environment

  - Telephone research mirrors many business processes and distribution networks

  - Mobile phones and mobile Internet means that research can use a range of methods to reach and stimulate respondents

CAPI: Disadvantages

- Costs particularly in b2b research may be high, but this must be offset against a higher response rate
- It can take a considerable amount of time to complete a survey
- Interviewers may be demotivated and may take short cuts to ensure that their quota of completed surveys is made
- Interview bias is a problem. Bias may affect

  Who is interviewed

  The way questions are asked

  The way an interviewer responds verbally and visually to an answer

  The way an answer is recorded
- Safety of interviewing staff may be an issue in some areas
- The training and control of field staff is important and adds to costs
- A dispersed sample geographically, for example regional store mangers, is clearly difficult to administer in this way and other data collection methods might need to be considered

CATI–Computer Assisted Interviewing, over the telephone

Advantages:

- CATI can facilitate the design administration and analysis of telephone interviewing
- Questionnaires can be customized and verbal comments can be recorded
- Inconsistencies can be highlighted and the researcher can probe to correct the inconsistency
- Automated dialling allows for efficient management of the interviewer
- Completely automated telephone interviews are more possible and may be used to capture simple research data, for example customer satisfaction data

Web-based Interviews

The use of 'Help me' buttons allow a pop-up dialogue screen in which questions can be asked and answered. 'Phone me' allows the respondent to be contacted by telephone and helped through the questionnaire.

Online Advantages:

- Cheap to administer, design, deliver and analyze
- Flexible in content and can include image and sound files
- Fast to administer and to report on
- Immediate and low-cost global reach
- Can replicate customer behaviour in both consumer and business markets
- Can be used automatically as pop up as a browser scrolls over a part of the web page
- Easy to control
- Can be completed at the respondent's convenience

Online Disadvantages:

- Technology may not be supported by all computers
- The amount of unsolicited e-mails or spam may affect perception of the questionnaire
- Samples might be difficult to construct
- It may be hard to validate who has responded

- People remain suspicious of the Internet and confidentiality needs to be ensured
- There may be a cost to the respondent if the questionnaire takes time to download
- The ease of use has led to very poor 'research' being carried out on an ad hoc basis

Postal Surveys

Advantages:

- Cheap
- Useful for geographically dispersed and larger samples
- Reduces interview bias
- Questionnaires can be piloted and revisions made
- Convenient
- Longer questionnaires can be delivered and completed effectively
- Allows respondents to confer and this may be desirable when researching high involvement purchases

Disadvantages:

- Response rate may be low
- Research design is limited
- Takes time to complete and this can lead to low response
- Availability of lists to form sample frames
- Limited control over the respondent
- High incidence of incomplete questionnaires or inconsistent answers
- Potential for bias in responders as only those who feel strongly may respond

Hints and Tips

- Quantitative research produces data that can be analyzed statistically

- Nearly everyone uses numbers and numerical relationships every day, even though there are stories that people do not know how to add and subtract well enough to check their change and that many of us have 'maths anxiety'

- Most people know more about quantitative reasoning than they think they do at first, and all of us are capable of amazing feats of calculation and reasoning, once we get the instruction that lets us in on the trick of it

- As you reflect on your quantitative skills, be sure to think about those skills that you use at work, at home, in education and in general, in order to identify your abilities in understanding, interpreting and using numerical information, charts and graphs, statistical information, formulas, and quantitative problem-solving techniques. You will be surprised!

- Statistics can demonstrate the strength of the relationship between different variables, i.e. how variables are correlated to each other. However, this is not the same as demonstrating a causal relationship

Go to www.cimvirtualinstitute.com and www.marketingonline.co.uk for additional support and guidance

QUESTIONNAIRE DESIGN

Syllabus Reference: 4.4, 4.5

After completing this unit you will be able to:

- Define the questionnaire
- Understand and outline the questionnaire design process
- Understand questionnaire formats
- Understand how to word a questionnaire
- Understand the issues in question sequencing
- Outline the role of piloting in the delivery of the questionnaire
- Outline the use of software packages to enable design of the questionnaire

Keywords

- Questionnaire – A structured data collection mechanism, involving a range of question formats and completed orally or in print. Questionnaires may be administered by interviewers or self completed by the respondent
- Coding – Turning responses into a form that enables analysis, usually by allocating a unique number to each response

Contd.

- Semantic differential – A scaling question that asks respondents to indicate the strength of their views, on normally a 5- or 7-point scale, between bipolar adjectives or statements
- Dichotomous questions – Questions for which there are two possible replies
- Forced scale – A scaling question that does not allow for a neutral response
- Likert scale – A scaling approach that asks respondents to indicate their strength of agreement, or disagreement, with a range of statements on a 5-point scale
- Scaling questions – Questions assigning numerical values to subjective concepts
- Skip questions – Questions that take respondents to other questions determined by the answer

The questionnaire design process

Wilson (2003) identifies a process for questionnaire development:

- Develop question topics
- Select question and response formats
- Determine sequence
- Design layout and appearance
- Pilot test
- Undertake the survey

What type of questions can be asked?

There are four main question types. These are:

- Closed questions – dichotomous
- Closed questions – multiple choice
- Open-ended
- Rating scales

closed Q is to ascertain facts

Closed questions – dichotomous

Simply, these are questions to which there are only two possible answers, e.g. yes and no. This sounds simple, but the question asked must fit into this answer structure.

Closed questions – multiple choice

It is important that, when multiple choice questions are being designed, the answers are mutually exclusive. Other issues with multiple choice responses include the number of potential responses. This may mean that the respondent cannot remember the first answers. In face-to-face interviews the responses may be put on a show card. This is not always possible in other media.

Open Q. invites the person to express themselves.

Open-ended questions

- Open-ended questions are questions in which an answer is not suggested. The respondent is free to respond in any way. The problem with open questions is analysis. If there are many categories of answers, then it may be hard to code the responses and it may reduce the effectiveness of the analysis

- One way around this is to pilot the survey and produce a pre-coded list of potential responses, which allows the interviewer to interpret the response and code it

- Open-ended questions can be very useful and the difficulties in managing them within a questionnaire are not huge. Their value can certainly outweigh these difficulties

Comparative versus non-comparative assessments

Comparative rating scales ask respondents to compare the organization or issues in relation to a common frame of reference. Non-comparative allows the respondents to select their own frame of reference.

Forced versus non-forced scales.

Forced scales do not allow a neutral position.

A forced scale:

Do you think that CIM courses are:

| Very inexpensive | Inexpensive | Expensive | Very expensive |

An unforced scale:

Do you think that CIM courses are:

| Very inexpensive | Inexpensive | Neither inexpensive nor expensive | Expensive | Very expensive |

Forced scales can be used when it is believed that there will be few neutral respondents. These are used also to force those who are in the neutral position to decide and can lead to spurious data being obtained.

Balanced versus Unbalanced scales

Balanced scales have a balanced number of positive and negative responses. Unbalanced may be used when piloting suggests that there will be fewer of any particular response and to explore the more common position with more sensitivity.

Number of Scale Positions

There are no hard and fast rules as to the number of positions on a scale. The most common number is 5. Some researchers use 7 or 9. The idea is that there is greater sensitivity in using a higher number.

Scales generally require at least two 'anchor' labels at each end of the scale. As we have seen earlier, it is also possible to label each position. It is also possible to use emoticons; smiley faces or thumbs up or down can be useful in certain markets and may be useful in international markets.

Commonly Used Scales

Respondents divide certain points or other units (possibly currency) between a number of attributes. This gives a rank order of attributes and an indication of the scale of difference between these attributes.

Likert Scales

The Likert scale asks respondents to indicate their level of agreement with a range of statements. Responses are scored from 1 to 5 and the result is an average score for each statement, indicating the level of agreement with the statement.

Figure 9.1 Likert scales

Semantic Differentials

Semantic differentials use words or statements and their opposites and measure the strength of opinion between them. The words are generated from exploratory or qualitative research

Expensive	1	2	3	4	5	Inexpensive
Effective	1	2	3	4	5	Ineffective
For career women	1	2	3	4	5	For the housewife
Modern	1	2	3	4	5	Old fashioned

Key
- Brand A
- Brand B

Semantic Differentials

Purchase intent scales

These scales are used to measure the respondents' intention to buy a product or a potential product. Example:

If this car was priced at £5999, would you:

Definitely buy	1
Probably buy	2
Probably not buy	3
Definitely not buy	4

Select Wording and Phrasing

The next stage of the questionnaire is to word the questions. At each stage of the process, the researcher should stop and ask 'Is the question really necessary?' Each question should be carefully evaluated on its own, in relation to other questions on the questionnaire and the overall objectives of the study. If the question does not contribute to the overall purpose of the research, it should not be included in the questionnaire.

Avoid:

- Ambiguity
- Two questions in one

- Leading or loaded questions
- Making assumptions
- Generalization
- Negative questions
- Hypothetical questions

Sequencing

- Wilson suggests that the questionnaires should be funnel sequenced, i.e. going from the broad to the narrow. The interviewer asks the most general questions about the subject and moves to narrower and more focused questions

Design, Layout and Appearance

The physical appearance of the questionnaire will determine levels of response, even if the questionnaire is interview-administered. It needs to be:

- Spaced effectively – it may save money but will reduce response
- Set in a serif type face. The serifs are the feet on the letters of a serif type face that keep the eye on the line; they are known to increase comprehension
- In at least 10 point font so that people can read the questionnaire
- Use skip and filter questions and routing instructions to help the respondent work through the questionnaire

Pilot

Piloting or testing the questionnaire is crucial

- It allows problems to be corrected
- Helps with the coding process
- Improves question sequencing
- Improves wording of questions

Questionnaire Checklist

- Are the objectives right?
- Will the data specified meet the objectives?
- Will the questions listed collect all the data required?
- Is every question essential?
- Will the right type of data be collected for: fact? opinion? motive?
- Is the question sequence logical?
- Are the types of questions being used appropriate: dichotomous? multiple-choice? open-ended? rating scales? Semantic differentials, Purchase intent scales.
- Is the question wording: simple to understand? unambiguous? clear?
- Is it reasonable to expect the respondent to answer every question?
- Will the answers be easy to record?
- Will the answers be easy to process?
- Does the questionnaire look good?
- Will it, and any show material, be easy for the interviewers to use?
- Has the questionnaire been piloted?
- Is the right type of questionnaire being used: personal? postal? telephone? online?

Source: Crouch and Housden, 2003

Hints and Tips

■ Go to the MRS website and download the document Questionnaire Design Guidelines

The process for construction of questionnaires follows these stages:

■ Develop question topics
■ Select question and response formats
■ Select wording
■ Determine sequence
■ Design layout and appearance
■ Pilot test
■ Undertake survey
■ Key aspects of layout are – spacing, quality of production, variety and coding/analysis requirements
■ Question types include – open-ended, closed, and scalar
■ Do get feedback on your initial list of questions. Feedback may be obtained from a small but representative sample of potential responders. A field trial of a tentative form of the questionnaire is also desirable

- Do locate personal or confidential questions at the end of the questionnaire. The early appearance of unsettling questions may result in respondents discontinuing the questionnaire

- Do order categories. When response categories represent a progression between a lower level of response and a higher one, it is usually better to list them from the lower level to the higher in left-to-right order, for example Try not to ask people to rank responses. They cannot be reasonably expected to rank more than about six things at a time, and many of them misinterpret directions or make mistakes in responding

- Look at the following websites:
  http://www.insitefulsurveys.com/survey-index6/ Designing-A-Questionnaires-.html
  http://www.dobney.com/ market_research.htm

Go to www.cimvirtualinstitute.com and www.marketingonline.co.uk for additional support and guidance

SAMPLING

Syllabus Reference: 4.6, 5.1

After completing this unit you will be able to:

- Define sampling
- Understand how to construct a sample for a survey
- Understand and identify the sampling process
- Understand and apply the statistical basis of sampling
- Understand and evaluate different sampling methods
- Understand the concepts of population, census and sample
- Understand how the sampling frame is constructed

Key definitions

- Sample – A part or subset of a population taken to be representative of the population as a whole
- Sampling frame – A list of the population of interest that is used to draw the sample in a survey
- Population – A population is the total number of people in any defined group of interest

Contd.

- Census – A survey of the entire population
- Confidence level – The probability that the true population value will fall within a known range
- Probability sampling – A sampling method that uses objective sample selection, so that every member of a population has a known probability of being selected
- Cluster sampling – A procedure in which clusters of population units are selected at random and then all or some of the units in the chosen clusters are studied
- Non-probability sampling – Non-probability sampling involves a subjective selection of respondents. Therefore, the probability of selecting respondents is unknown
- Sample error – The error in a survey caused by using a sample to estimate the value of a parameter in the population
- Systematic sampling – A probability sampling method, in which respondents are selected using a 1 in 'n' approach
- Stratified random sampling – A probability sampling method, in which the sample is forced to contain respondents from each of the key segments of a population
- Standard deviation – A measurement of dispersion that calculates the average distance of the values in a data set from the mean value
- Snowball sampling – A type of non-probability sampling, where initial respondents are selected at random and subsequent respondents are then selected by referrals or information from the earlier respondents

Wilson (2003) highlights five key questions that inform the sampling process:

1. We need to understand the nature of the people we wish to survey
2. We need to know where they are
3. We need to know how we select them
4. We need to know the number of people we wish to survey
5. We need to understand how representative this sample is of the population as a whole

What is a Sample?

Sampling is used to make an estimate of the characteristics of the population as a whole. Sampling overcomes the impossibility in almost every market of asking all members of a population their opinion.

The sampling process. Wilson (2003) outlines a six-stage sampling process:

- Define the population of interest
- Determine whether to sample or census
- Select the sampling frame
- Choose a sampling method
- Determine the sample size
- Implement the sampling procedure

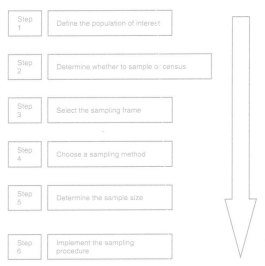

Figure 10.1 The sampling process

Sampling Methods

There are two broad sampling methods:

Probability sampling

The key characteristic is that every member of the population of interest has a known chance of being selected, independent of any subjective selection by the researcher.

Four commonly used methods of probability sampling:

- Simple random sampling
- Systematic sampling
- Stratified random sampling   men vs. women / user vs no-user
- Cluster sampling

Simple Random Sampling

Each member of the population has an equal chance of being selected for the survey. Members are randomly selected by a computerized random number generator or tables until the required sample size is filled.

Stratified Random Sampling

This method divides the population into two or more **mutually exclusive groups, e.g.** men or women, users or non-users of a product, and takes random samples from within them, using either of the methods above.

Cluster sampling

Cluster sampling is a procedure in which clusters of population units are selected at random and then all or some of the units in the chosen clusters are studied. The technique works when a population can easily be divided into representative clusters, e.g. in membership directories.

Non-Probability Sampling

Examples of non-probability sampling are:

Convenience sampling

Based on the convenience of the researcher.

Judgement or purposive sampling

The researcher consciously selects a sample considered appropriate for the study. This may be based on certain companies representing a sector. The market might include all major department stores in the sample, as well as a random selection of other outlets.

Quota Sampling

Is defined by ESOMAR as 'A type of non-probability sample where the required number of units with particular characteristics are specified.' This is based on the idea that, if known characteristics of the population are reproduced in the same proportion in the sample, it is representative of that population; e.g. age, sex and social class can be used to select quotas.

Advantages of quota sampling include:

- Speed and cost
- Allows sampling to take place where a sample frame may not be available but key characteristics of the population are known – e.g. in overseas b2b research
- Interviewers do not have to interview named individuals, they are screened in or out via a small number of classification questions
- The data, when compared to random methods which are perhaps double the cost, has been proven to be acceptable, provided that the research is managed effectively
- Cost savings may be used to improve the quality of research, through increasing sample sizes or using a different method in support of the survey
- Its popularity shows that it works!

Disadvantages include:

- Whilst known characteristics may be distributed in correct proportions, unknown characteristics that may be relevant to the survey may not be. Hidden bias may exist that is not discovered
- Researchers may be biased as to the type of respondents they choose to interview

Snowball Sampling

It is defined by ESOMAR (2005) as 'A type of non-probability sampling where initial respondents are selected at random and subsequent respondents are then selected by referrals or information from the earlier respondents'.

This is very useful in markets where there is low incidence of the population – in b2b markets, where buyers of competitive intelligence or where unusual behaviour is under consideration.

Online issues

The same methods can be used in online research but the problem is that sample frames are less available. A range of panels have been set up to counter this, for example Nielsen net ratings.

Determining the Sample Size

There is no necessary relationship between the size of the population and the sample. Whilst the larger the sample size the more accurate the results, this has to be traded off against the cost of producing this effect and the complexity, and therefore cost of managing the collection and processing of large amounts of data.

The cost of producing more response is normally proportional, that is the percentage increase in the cost of producing a percentage increase in sample size will be the same. However, the increase in accuracy is not proportional. Sampling error tends to decrease at a rate equal to the square root of the relative increase in sample size. A sample increased by 100 percent will improve accuracy by 10 percent.

Other Factors That are Relevant to Determining Sample Size

- **Budget** – always a factor in marketing decisions; the higher the sample size, the greater the cost
- **Timings** – the larger the sample size, the longer it takes to gather data and complete the analysis
- **The risk attached to any decision** – the greater the risk, the higher the level of accuracy required
- The nature of the research may indicate complex analysis of sub-samples, for example women as opposed to men buying a certain product; if this is the case the sub-samples need to be large enough to ensure statistical reliability

Hints and Tips

- It is important to understand in what circumstances and for what purposes different approaches to sampling are used

- The objectives of the research will determine the type of sample that is needed, e.g. are the views of a particular sub-set of the population required, or are the views of a representative group of the whole population needed?

- Companies spend a lot of money trying to identify and reach sections of the population from which profitable customers can be drawn. Effective sampling for research can contribute to this objective

Go to www.cimvirtualinstitute.com and www.marketingonline.co.uk for additional support and guidance

QUANTITATIVE DATA ANALYSIS

Syllabus Reference: 4.6, 5.1

After completing this unit you will be able to:

- Understand the process of data management, entry, editing, coding and cleaning
- Understand concepts of tabulation and statistical analysis
- Understand the main techniques of statistical analysis, including descriptive statistics, statistical significance and hypotheses testing, the measurement of relationships and multivariate analysis
- Understand the use of computer packages that can help with the process

Key definitions

- Coding – The process that allocates a number to each answer and it is this that allows analysis to take place
- Interval data – Similar to ordinal data, but with the added dimension that intervals between the values on a scale are equal
- Ratio data – Actual or real numbers that have a meaningful or absolute zero

Contd.

- Factor analysis – Studies the relationships between variables to simplify data into a smaller set of composite variables or factors
- Cross tabulations – Table setting out responses to one question relative to others
- Coefficient of determination – Measure of the strength of linear relationship between a dependent and an independent variable
- Conjoint analysis – Analysis that asks respondents to make decisions between various attributes measuring their relative importance
- Chi square – A test measuring the goodness of fit between the observed sample values and the expected distribution of those values
- Z Test – A hypothesis test about a single mean where the sample is greater than 30
- T Test – A hypothesis test about a single mean where the sample is less than 30
- Null hypothesis – The hypothesis that is tested
- Least squares – A regression method that produces a line of best fit for a data set involving a dependent and independent variable
- Independent variable – A variable that has influence on the value of the dependent variable
- Dependent variable – The response measure studied
- Regression – Examines the relationship between two variables

Introduction

The analysis of data is a key skill of the marketing manager. An ability to understand basic methods of data analysis is useful. Data analysis can be done easily now, using computer packages such as Excel and SPSS.

Editing and Coding

Before data is processed, it is assessed for completeness and coherence. The editing process involves computer or manual checking of the data, to look for respondent or interview errors or inconsistencies.

Coding is the process that allocates a number to each answer and it is this that allows analysis to take place. Coding open questions involves using a sample of the completed questionnaires and developing a coding frame, or a list of codes for all possible responses to an open question.

Data Entry

Data entry may be carried out automatically through CAPI, CAWI and CATI systems, or scanned into the computer using optical character recognitions software, or they may be entered by hand. Once this is complete, the data can be analyzed.

Tabulation and Statistical Analysis

There are four types of data that can be analyzed:

Nominal Data

These refer to values that are given to objects that, in themselves, have no intrinsic numerical value. For example, we assigned a value to gender: 1 for men and 2 for women.

We can count them and create percentages.

Ordinal Data

These data represent rank order data. They do not imply that there is an equal gap between items ranked and there is no other meaning to them other than rank order.

Interval Data

It is rank order data in which the intervals between the data are equal. These are also known as interval scales. Interval scales rank elements relative to each other, but not from any observable origin. This means that the data has its meaning only by virtue of the comparison between elements selected.

Ratio Data

Ratio data has an absolute zero or observable origin. For example, shoe size, products bought, or age. This means all analyses are possible.

Tabulations, Whole Counts and Frequency

Tables give researchers a feel for data. Frequency distributions are simply counts of the numbers of respondents who gave each possible answer to a particular question. They are used to help the researcher form the next stage of analysis.

Cross Tabulations (cross tabs)

These tables 'cross' the answers to one question with the answers to another, for example age of respondent and products purchased.

Descriptive Statistics

These data are used to give the researcher a view of the location of the data and its spread. These are known as measures of central tendency and measures of dispersion or variability. Measures of central tendency indicate typical values for data sets. These are the mean, median and mode. The mean is the arithmetic average. The mode is the value in a set of data that appears most frequently. A data set may have more than one mode – a number of categories may be equal and share the highest frequency.

Measures of Dispersion

These indicate how spread out or dispersed a data set is. They include the range, variance and standard deviation. The range is the interval from the highest to the lowest value in a data set. Variance is a measure of how spread out a data set is, and we work it out by looking at the average squared deviation of each number from its mean.

Hypothesis Testing

A hypothesis is an assumption about a characteristic in the population.

Research will allow the researcher to conclude something about the population.

The testing of hypothesis follows a simple structure.

There are two forms of hypotheses:

(a) The Null hypothesis or H0 is the one that will be tested, that is, the existing situation where no difference is expected

(b) The Alternative hypothesis or H1 is the one in which a difference is expected.

Statistical Significance

There are advantages to using samples rather than collecting data from the whole population. However, the data from a sample will always be subject to error. There may be a mathematical difference between the results from a sample compared with those from the whole population but, if after applying significance tests, the difference is shown not to have occurred through chance or error, then it is regarded as statistically significance.

Significance Tests

These measure whether the difference between two percentages is significant or not, or whether the difference between two means from different samples is significant. In order to carry out these tests three concepts must be considered. There are a range of significance tests available and the most frequently used are:

- Chi-square test
- Z test
- T Test

Degrees of Freedom

Degrees of freedom are used to reflect potential bias in an example.

Independent versus Related Samples

Selection of an appropriate test technique may involve considering whether samples are independent or related. In related samples, the measurement of the variable of interest in one sample might affect the measurement of the variable of interest in another.

Errors in Hypothesis Testing

Two types of error are known – type one and type two. A concept called the alpha level defines the probability of committing such an error and is commonly set at 0.05 or a 5 percent chance of the error occurring.

Type one errors happen when the null hypothesis is rejected when it is true. Type two errors mean accepting the null hypothesis when it is false. Reducing the alpha level increases the chance of a type one error occurring.

The Chi Square Test

This measures whether the differences in cross tabulated data sets are significant. This is also known as 'goodness of fit' between observed distribution and expected distribution of the variable. It compares one or more sets of data to indicate if there is a real difference.

Hypotheses About Means

Where sample data produces a mean or a proportion, researchers can use a Z or a T test to test hypotheses relating to them. Z tests are used if the researcher is aware of the population's mean and variance. This may be the real mean or variance, or assumed figures. The sample must be higher than 30. T tests are used if the mean and variance are unknown or if a sample is less than 30. T tests are more frequently used by researchers. They allow the researcher to work out if the difference between the two averages is real or significant, or simply due to the fact that the figures are derived from a sample. For example, if a customer-satisfaction survey ranks one brand higher than average, is this a real difference or due to a sampling error?

Measuring Relationships

Correlation and Regression

These techniques measure the degree of association between two variables such as income and number of foreign holidays or customer satisfaction and product repurchase, or advertising spend and sales.

Bivariate techniques measure the relationship between two variables. This does not prove that one variable causes the other but rather indicates the degree of relationship between the variables. Often a cause-and-effect link is assumed but this is not a proven relationship. It is important to apply common sense in the interpretation of the results.

Variables are labelled dependent and independent. Independent variables are those assumed to influence the dependent variable.

There are two types of correlation analysis. Pearson's product movement correlation is used with interval and ratio data. It produces a correlation coefficient which can have a maximum value of þ1 and a minimum value of −1.

Perfect positive correlation between two sets of variables is indicated by þ1. This means that if there is a movement of 5 percent on one variable, it is accompanied by a movement in the same direction of 5 percent on another variable. For example, when satisfaction increases by 5 percent, sales rise by 5 percent.

Perfect negative correlation means the two variables have a perfect negative relationship. If for every 10 percent increase in price the sales volume decreased by 10 percent, then the correlation coefficient would be −1.

When changes in one variable are not associated with changes in the other variable, the correlation coefficient will be calculated as zero.

Generally, correlation coefficients above þ0.7 or below −0.7 are believed to show an increasing degree of association. This might require further research to explore the association in more detail from larger samples.

When ordinal data is being considered, Spearman's rank order correlation is used. This might be used to compare ranking of companies' promotional expenditure with a ranking of their sales turnover.

Low coefficients do not mean that there is no association. It only implies absence of a linear association. It may be that a non-linear association exists.

Simple Regression Analysis

- Regression analysis is concerned with dependence. For example, sales volume may be predicted based on other variables. The allocation of dependent and independent variables is more important in regression analysis. Movement in the dependent variables depends upon movement in the independent variables

- Sales forecasters use regression analysis. However, it is clear that the movement in a market is caused by a number of factors and this is dealt with through multivariate techniques, which we will look at later

Least Squares

This is the most common approach to regression. Least squares identifies a line of best fit between observations and this enables an estimated regression function that indicates the relationship. Simple regression analysis may be enhanced through the coefficient of determination. This measures the strength of the relationship between variables.

Factor Analysis

Factor analysis reduces a large number of variables to a more manageable smaller set of factors, based on the interrelationships between them. It provides insight for the groupings that emerge and allows for more efficient analysis of complex data.

Cluster Analysis

This technique groups objects or respondents into mutually exclusive and exhaustive groups. The technique is often used in data base marketing to create segments, based on behaviour across a range of variables.

Multidimensional Scaling or Perceptual Mapping

Consumers rate objects, often brands, by the relative strength of an attribute compared to other objects or brands. This creates a perception of a 'position' in the market and is very useful for determining brand perception and repositioning.

Conjoint Analysis

Conjoint analysis is a way of looking at customers' decisions as a trade-off between multiple attributes in products or services. In conjoint analysis, consumers are asked to make decisions about various attributes, trading lower price for comfort, for example, in car purchases.

Software Packages

There are many software packages on the market that will do most of this for you.

The key thing is to understand what these packages will do to your valuable data and to produce efficient analysis, which allows a focus on the research problem. Excel is adequate for most of the key formulae outlined above, but there are specialists; perhaps the best known software packages include:
SPSS www.spss.com and SNAP www.mercator.co.uk

Hints and Tips

■ Market metrics are used in business planning and marketing monitoring to keep the marketing programme on track. The most common market metrics that companies use are:

Market size
Market share
Market penetration
Installed base
Product usage
Customer attitudes
Brand awareness
Advertising awareness
Brand image
Customer satisfaction

■ Quantitative surveys mean getting people to answer fixed questions in questionnaires. Because the objective is measurement, it is important that all people answer the same question

Go to www.cimvirtualinstitute.com and www.marketingonline.co.uk for additional support and guidance

PRESENTING MARKETING RESEARCH

Unit 12

After completing this unit you will be able to:

- Identify the structure for the presentation of a research report
- Outline the key features of an oral presentation
- Know how to make the most of a presentation
- Understand the use of graphics in presentation of data

Key definitions

- Oral presentation – A verbal presentation of research findings, using a range of supporting material
- Executive summary – A precise of the report

The final report to the client is perhaps the most important part of the research planning process.

Research report format

- Title page
- Contents
- Executive summary
- Introduction
- Situation analysis and problem definition
- Research methodology and limitations
- Findings and analysis
- Conclusions and recommendations
- Appendices

Research has shown that people forget:

- 30 percent of what you tell them after just 3 hours
- 90 percent after only 3 days

Visual aids can help and variety is the key. The combination of verbal and visual material has been shown to deliver 85 percent recollection after 3 hours and up to 65 percent after 3 days.

Problems in presentations

Wilson (2003) presents a list of common problems in presenting reports:

- Assuming understanding: there is insufficient background and interpretation given to results
- Excessive length
- Unrealistic recommendations which are commercially naive
- Spurious accuracy: results are based on too small sample sizes
- Obscure statistics: a range of obscure techniques may not be useful
- Over elaborate presentation: too many graphics may obscure more than it reveals

Presentation tips

- Meet your objectives. State them early on and show throughout how your presentation contributes to their achievement. You might even ask the audience what their objectives are at the beginning of the presentation, note them on a flip chart and at the end of the presentation tick them off

- Know your audience; what do they want to hear? How many will be present? Who are they? What positions do they hold?

- How will you dress? Is it formal or informal or will you be overdressed in a suit and a tie?

- What do your audience expect?

- Keep it brief and to the point, do not use too many tables and graphs. Use a balanced mixture of words and images. Keep to time

- Be prepared for interruptions and stop presenting if your audience are distracted. Do not plough on

- Turn off mobile phones and ask your audience to do the same. Try to manage the physical characteristics of the room, heat and lighting, and air conditioning

- If using PowerPoint technology, make sure that it is compatible with the projection system. Make sure that your slides do not contain too much information and that tables and graphics can be read

- During the presentation, maintain eye contact with your audience. Try to avoid having a physical barrier between you and your audience
- Be aware of your body language, relax your shoulders, smile and try to project enthusiasm
- Relax and use natural movements. Engage with your audience but do not invade their personal space
- Make eye contact with all people in the room early in the presentation – get them on your side
- Face your audience rather than the screen. If you are able to, determine where each member of the team presenting and the audience will sit
- Never turn your back to the audience
- Do not hide behind lecterns and A4 notes
- Use cue cards if necessary, do not try to ad lib unless you are well rehearsed
- Provide handouts for your audience of the slides, tables and graphs that may be hard to read
- Keep to time and take responsibility for your own timings. Some audiences for competitive pitches will stop a presentation if it overruns
- Use pictures, video and audio clips to enliven and add variety to the presentation, but do not make a presentation over busy

- Liven it up by using a variety of support and dynamic pacing through the presentation.
  - Flipchart
  - Overhead projector slides
  - PowerPoint
  - Story boards
  - Video and sound clips
- Practise, practise, practise, remember 'fail to prepare, prepare to fail'
  - Make sure you carry out a 'dress' rehearsal. Practise speaking out loud
  - Practise all aspects of the presentation including the transition between speakers and the use of supporting technology or audio-visual aids
- Tell them what you will tell them, tell them and tell them what you have told them
- Structure the presentation and use staging posts and summarizing slides to close sections and introduce new sections
- Always start and finish on a high note
- Do not be shy about saying that you want the business

Hints and Tips

Presenting market research results orally involves:

- Understanding your audience and responding to their needs
- Structuring the presentation – Introduction, Methodology, Key findings, Conclusions and recommendations, and Questions
- Delivering the presentation confidently and professionally
- Presenting data appropriately using tables and charts
- There are common mistakes to be avoided, including:

  Assuming prior knowledge

  Presenting for too long

  Misleading about accuracy or with statistics

  Distracting the audience from the key message through technology

  Relying solely on technology that might not work

- Look at the following website www.presentationbiz.co.uk/articles/ articles_general.htm

Go to www.cimvirtualinstitute.com and www.marketingonline.co.uk for additional support and guidance